CONOCIMIENTOS

PRESS

SOJOURNERS
TO
JOKE SINGS

TALES OF
CHINATOWN & BEYOND

RON LEE

with

L K LENNIE LEE

CONOCIMIENTOS

PRESS

Book design by ash good.

Published by Conocimientos Press, LLC
San Antonio, Texas

ISBN: 978-1-961-794-06-1

Dedicated to Grandma and Grandpa Lee

Lin Kim Lennie Lee & Harry Pang Lee

CONTENTS

FOREWORD *by Dr. Hertha D. Sweet Wong* 5

PREFACE: *The Evolution of a Book* 9

INTRODUCTION: *Bruce Lee v Grandma Lee* 11

PART I—A SIX-HUNDRED YEAR ODYSSEY
CHAPTER 1   In the Beginning 19
CHAPTER 2   Coming to America 27
CHAPTER 3   Ha Liu Chune 31
CHAPTER 4   Gum San 33
CHAPTER 5   Jub Gwuck 36
CHAPTER 6   China Beach 41

PART II—THE MAVERICK
CHAPTER 7   Chow Chong 51
CHAPTER 8   Robert Louis Stevenson or "RLS" 56
CHAPTER 9   The Extraordinary Junk 69
CHAPTER 10 Wild West Stories 75
CHAPTER 11 Little Pete Must Die 85
CHAPTER 12 Filial Piety 89

PART III – LENNIE'S STORY
CHAPTER 13 Badasses 101
CHAPTER 14 Suey Ying Tong Memories 107
CHAPTER 15 The Babysitter 111
CHAPTER 16 1934: Home at Last 116
CHAPTER 17 Escape from Slavery 119
CHAPTER 18 Rags to Riches 123
CHAPTER 19 When Harry met Lennie 127
CHAPTER 20 Becoming Mrs. Lee 130

PART IV—CHINATOWN LIFE

CHAPTER 21 Nam Chung Music Club 137

CHAPTER 22 A Multicultural Place 148

CHAPTER 23 Narm Bo Mo Bay Khoun—Sewing Factories. . 154

CHAPTER 24 Mol Ha Paw—Shrimp Shelling Women . . . 170

CHAPTER 25 The Cigar Makers 174

CHAPTER 26 Laundries 187

PART V—JOKE SING STORIES

CHAPTER 27 Pacific Grove & Mendocino 201

PART VI—FAMILY TIES

CHAPTER 28 The Merchant 219

CHAPTER 29 High Tech Joke Sings 228

CHAPTER 30 The Chans 231

EPILOGUE: *A Woman of Courage & Determination*
. 237

FOREWORD

Sometime in the early 1990s, shortly after I arrived at the University of California Berkeley's English Department as an Assistant Professor, an older woman came to my office hours. She had noticed that I was teaching a course on Autobiography and one on Translating Orality (obtaining, transcribing, and then translating oral narratives into written ones). She explained that she was working on her family history: a combination of stories she had heard from elder relatives and her own personal stories of growing up in San Francisco's Chinatown. She asked if she could audit my classes and whether I'd be willing to give her feedback on her work. My answer to both was yes. That was my first encounter with Lennie Lee, someone I came to know as a woman of tenacity and clarity.

Although her auditing didn't last throughout the semester, we met regularly for several months. Often, she brought me the fruits of her latest research, sometimes from microfiche copies of old Chinese newspapers that I was (then and now) incapable of reading. She interviewed numerous relatives, recounted family stories she'd been told as a child, researched various archives in Chinatown and throughout San Francisco and traveled to China many times to research her family's pre-immigration experience.

A retired high school teacher, Lennie Lee was a scholar of intense focus and clear purpose. Not only was she intent to tell her individual story (of living in Chinatown from the 1920s through the 1950s before moving nearby where she remained to the end of her 98 years) and including her family's story (that goes back to their arrival in the 1840s, pre-dating the Gold Rush, and before the Ming Dynasty). Her focus was on the experience of her family immigrating from China to San Francisco and of the transformative process of learning a new language and culture under shifting, but unrelenting xenophobic hostility. She did not shy away from the dangers, hardships, and challenges, and she noted moments of generosity, grace, and humor.

Her stories range from accounts of terrifyingly racist atrocities (her father's and granduncle's story of the teakwood coffins being delivered to San Francisco only to be attacked by a drunken mob of White men who murdered stowaways inside the coffins) to anecdotes of adventure narratives (in which Lennie's ancestor's seafaring stories were perhaps the inspiration for Robert Louis Stevenson's *Treasure Island)* to tales of Tong power struggles (the assassination of Fong Ching known as "Little Pete") to stories of the challenges of everyday life (the ways in which life was especially dangerous for Chinese girls and women).

About thirty years later, I received an email from an unknown source. It turned out to be Lennie's son, Ron Lee, who had learned about his mother's work with me so long ago. I agreed happily to read various versions of the manuscript, to talk through his vision for it. During this time, as I was clearing out my office, I came across a manila envelope filled with newspaper articles and notes Lennie had sent me. I shared these with Ron. I have enjoyed watching Lennie's project change and develop over the past few years, just as I've enjoyed getting to know Ron and Lucretia.

So here it is. Lennie's project of bearing witness to pass on to her children and grandchildren, enhanced by her son and granddaughters.

When editing and shaping Lennie's stories, her son Ron, along with his daughters and nephews, offered their own research, commentary, and context. A transgenerational family history that illuminates many individuals and their sets of relationships and that highlights numerous modes of survival through fishing and shrimping, cigar making, sewing, doing laundry, and generally, learning to live by one's wits—this is the end-result. Finally, despite many generational iterations of racism, Lennie and Ron and Ron's daughters shed light on Chinese immigrant and Chinese American citizen resilience and endurance, helping us to rethink the history of Chinese

Americans, from those who came with a plan to earn money and return to China to those who remained to become Americans, from *Sojourners* to *Joke Sings*.

—Hertha D. Sweet Wong
Professor Emerita of English
University of California, Berkeley

PREFACE
The evolution of a book

Sojourners to *Joke Sings: Tales of Chinatown & Beyond* was the result of sorting through documents and writings left by my mother. Amateur historian and anthropologist, L K Lennie Lee collected histories and stories about her ancestral roots and the community. Through her journals and writing, we found out that our family matriarch, L K Lennie Lee (1923-2021) had written a family history titled *Joke Sings*. She provided her reasons for writing.

> *Joke Sings is a story told by an American-born grand-mother, for her four Lee grandchildren, as to what life was like growing-up in an old-segregated Chinatown during the 1920s-50s, and the stories I heard from my elders.*

Joke Sing or Jook Sing—in the Mandarin language—is a Chinese term that describes people who have opted to become American. While this may be complacent today, it wasn't in the 1840s when my forebears first arrived. Back then, the objective was to make some money and return to China.

With my two daughters and two nephews, I dutifully went about reviewing L K Lennie Lee's work. The intention was that after a little bit of editing, I would pass out copies of the book at a Celebration of Life—the life of Lennie Lee. Upon reviewing the materials compiled and left by my mother, I found an autobiography, framed inside a memoir containing vivid descriptions of life in San Francisco's Chinatown.

I was astonished at the adventurous lives my ancestors led. There were stories about seafaring, and tales that defied beliefs that could possibly advance notions that our ancestors were the initial inspiration for Robert Louis Stevenson's (RLS) iconic adventure novel *Treasure Island*.

Outside of Lennie Lee's narratives, there are no textbooks that corroborate the heretofore untold tales. Thus, it was left to the grandchildren and me to review the evidence. After three years of research, we concluded that Lennie Lee's stories expounded on events such as the 1882 Chinese Exclusion Act.

While most readers may be enticed by our family connection to RLS, for us, it was not about whom we knew. Thus, I present our ancestral legacy that brings the family's all-time adventures to light, narrating stories of the first Chinese settlers in America—the Joke Sings.

With the answers more questions emerged. However, as the living author and supported by the literary and historical artifacts left by Lennie Lee, my aim is to make our ancestral history visible. Along with her story, I link the commonalities in our lived experiences and incorporate our Chinese connections to San Francisco, Stockton, Sacramento, and the Monterey Bay.

This book reflects Lennie's use of terms in the language she maintained. For instance, "Joke Sing" is more often referred to as "Jook Sing." However, she didn't write Chinese and spoke an unusual dialect of her peasant heritage. To validate and honor her knowledge, language terms appear as she wrote them, so that the reader may decipher them phonetically. Doing this does not change anything about the stories that follow, rather they authenticate the cultural and linguistic knowledge that L K Lennie Lee carried, and that her progeny inherited.

A note she wrote at the top of the first page inspired me to explore her stories. *"Grandmother Lee's Autobiography. Note: Needs Corrections and upgrading."* For this reason, our book documents my mother's stories in her own words and her narrative is italicized to record and authenticate her voice.

After a long productive life *"Grandma Lee"* quietly passed away at the age of ninety-eight. It was after her death that we came upon her book, while going through her belongings.

INTRODUCTION
Bruce Lee vs. Grandma Lee

"Uncle Ron, look at what grandma wrote.
It reads like an episode of *Warrior*."

—ERIK, LENNIE'S GRANDSON AND RON'S NEPHEW

From the journals and written material left by LK Lennie Lee née Chow, my nephew Erik found a binder with a lime green cover titled *Joke Sing*—a term that describes a Chinese person who identifies as American. It was written by my mother, Erik's grandmother.

"What's *Warrior*?"

That was my only response, being unfamiliar with contemporary culture. I learned that this was a TV series based on an eight page "treatment" written by Bruce Lee in the 1970s. The setting was San Francisco's Chinatown in the late 1870s. As was to be expected, the series contained a string of fight scenes between individuals and organizations. In that series, there were side stories, mostly with salacious themes.

I joked it was unlikely she and Bruce would share stories in common. I was wrong—the first page of L K Lennie Lee's journal read,

> *My father Chow Chong told me that he had just returned from Kwong Hoy Seaport, Hoy Sun (Taishan County), Canton (Quangdong) province, China, with a load of carved teakwood coffins my Granduncle Ning Choie Tane had ordered. ... teakwood coffins ... for Chinatown funeral parlors and ... those who wanted the bodies of their deceased sent to China. My father and Granduncle Choie Tane were already on the wharf getting their horse and cart ready to load the coffins in which they had hidden Chinese stowaways before the ship had docked.*

Unemployed White unionists, aroused by rumors that the returning Chinese seamen had again brought stowaways, slaughtered them in their coffins… To make an example of them, the drunken Whites … nailed the coffins tightly shut. Then they hammered extra-long railroad spikes through the tops of the coffins down into the bodies of the stowaways.

The White killers continued drinking and celebrating as they listened to the dying Chinese scream and thrash about. The murderous rampage ended with the Whites beating up the Chinese seamen still on board; a number of them were thrown into the San Francisco Bay. My father and Granduncle Choie Tane escaped during the rampage … as they were on the wharf getting their horse and cart ready to pick up the coffins.

Bruce Lee couldn't have imagined such a narrative. I read LK's journals and was astonished to find stories about a famous murder, mystery and intrigue, escape from slavery, seafaring adventures, buried "treasures," and rags to riches stories.

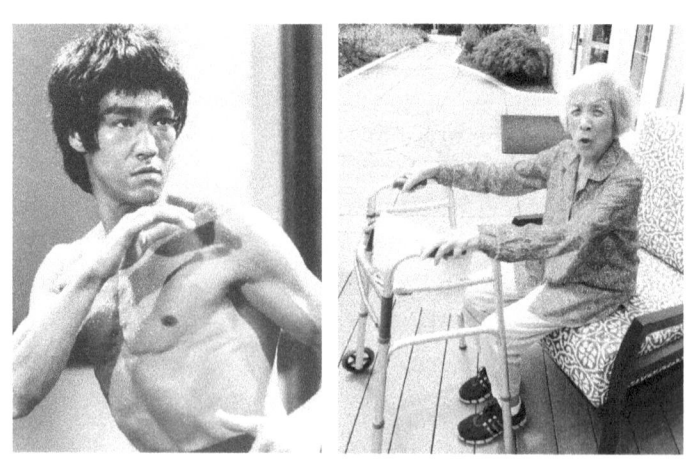

BRUCE LEE VERSUS GRANDMA LEE

Bruce Lee, photograph from Enter The Dragon *by Michael Ochs courtesy of Getty Images.*
L K Lennie Lee, photo courtesy Ron Lee.

To search for a Lee connection, I watched the series for comparison. Set in San Francisco's Chinatown in 1878, the main character, Ah Sahm, is a martial arts master who joins a Tong and fights his way through a series of adventures. Other characters are based loosely, taking liberties about those who actually were alive. Labor unrest, crooked politicians and policemen, bawdy activities, and Tong fighting took place, although the show is fictional. Except for an Irish person, most were interesting characters to follow.

Unfortunately, the creators of the program erred when this man was portrayed as somewhat sympathetic. In reality, he was one of the most racists xenophobes in California history. It is safe to assume Bruce Lee did not base the fictional Dylan Leary on Denis Kearney. The corresponding true-life person in *Joke Sings* would be Chow Chong (1865-1943) Lennie's father, my grandfather.

In real life, Chong—in Chinese cultural practice surnames are given first—dealt with many of the situations found in *Warrior* without resorting to martial arts which he did not practice. Nevertheless, he traveled without incident, well outside the confines of Chinatown, something extremely dangerous to do.

Most Chinese immigrants, despite rampant racism or the fear and hatred of foreigners and open discrimination, were not combative. Instead, they followed an ancient concept called "Eating Bitterness" (吃苦—chi ku), which means to persevere through hardship without complaint. Suffering might've even been considered a virtue.

Chinese people weren't necessarily timid, just non-confrontational. Their goal was to earn money and return to the homeland. They had strong opinions that were expressed only to family and friends—a type of stoicism. On the other hand, the decision to become a Joke Sing could be fraught with difficulties. In the early days, both Chinese and the majority societies would've looked down on such people. What is the opposite of Eating Bitterness? Was there a special trait the Joke Sing had? The term "badass" comes to mind. The concept has variant connotations, both good and bad.

Dictionaries offer definitions of the term and the one that fits Lennie's description best is badass—a noun describing "someone who deals bravely with difficult situations." The Clan and Lennie were badass, and Bruce Lee is often regarded as an all-time one.

Adventure stories like those told by Bruce Lee and the creators of *Warrior* reflect but one aspect of the many stories Lennie wrote. Her writings document how she avoided being sold into slavery as a young girl. She wrote about the ways one becomes highly successful. Also, Lennie made connections to our ancestors' military legacy in the Ming Dynasty, writing about incredible seafaring adventures, and detailing descriptions of life in Chinatown contesting the veneer of tourism. Bruce Lee, who was born in San Francisco, would've loved those stories.

L K Lenie Lee was not as forthcoming about family history, although deeply invested in Chinese American history and culture. Her distancing may be attributed to strained relationships she had with her mother when she was young and my father's questionable immigration status.

Oral histories collected by my mother greatly display her vast knowledge, along with an extraordinary ability to recall events, and the many situations she witnessed or heard about as a child. L K Lennie Lee was serious minded and not given to hyperbole. Her writing was overseen by two University of California, Berkeley professors, one in Asian American Studies and the other in English—Emerita English Professor Hertha D Sweet Wong, who wrote the forward.

Among the written material my daughters, nephews, and I sorted out, there was much information collected, and we soon found enough material for the book. I did the bulk of the writing, as the Covid-19 crisis facilitated the process as my wife, Lucretia and I did not venture out of the house, and I had time on my hands. I wasn't sure I was up to the herculean task of writing a book much less publishing one. Then, at one point, I came across a quote by Charlie Chin affiliated with the Chinese Historical Society of America. He wrote, *"Major immigration did not start until the passage of the 1965 Civil Rights Act, 90 percent of Asian American and Pacific Islanders are unaware of their histories" (See Wikimedia, https://en.wikipedia.ogr wiki History of Chinese Americans np).*

JOKE SINGS

L K Lennie Lee left me an awe-inspiring gift. Through her treasured stories I expand upon what historians claim to be the presence of Chinese in America since the mid-1800s, or as sociologist Paul Siu (1959) named them *sojourners*, whose intentions were to come to Gum San or Gold Mountain to earn money and send it home. Their dream was to become rich, but their obligation always was to return.

However, if one should perish, custom dictated that remains be sent back to their native village for burial. To stay would have been out of the question. Sojourners would've had family duty to fulfill their obligations. It was often the case that they were married, had children, and extended family left behind, all counting on income that would be sent home.

On a few occasions, some opted to stay, and, on rarer instances, others found a way to start families. It was this second group that was cast in opposition to sojourners, and were not viewed positively, and given the term Joke Sing—a pejorative and demeaning concept that translates to bamboo pole. This metaphor implies that water poured into hollow bamboo stops flowing at the nodes and remains there. To Lennie, the concept referred to a person who became fully included in American society but retained characteristics of their Asian heritage. She considered it a term of pride.

According to Lennie, my forebears were an unusual kind of Joke Sing. They left Kwong Hoy, China, in the early 1840s, before the Gold Rush, with the intent of staying in America. They likely settled in Yerba Buena later named San Francisco.

What follows chronicles an odyssey that began during the Ming Dynasty (1368-1644) and continues to this day. My daughters Meredith and Alison, sixth generation San Franciscans, still live in the City or what locals call San Francisco. Also, there's a seventh-generation cousin.

PART I

A SIX-HUNDRED YEAR ODYSSEY

ORIGINALLY A SEAFARING AND ENTERPRISING
PEOPLE WHOSE DREAMS WERE TO ADVANCE IN
LIFE, THEY NAVIGATED THE SOUTH SEA PATHS
TO ESCAPE THE ECONOMIC HARDSHIPS OF WAR.
KNOWLEDGEABLE OF SEA CURRENTS AND FINDING
THEMSELVES INSIDE THIS DEPRESSED ECONOMY,
CHINESE PEOPLE JOURNEYED TO GUM SAN OR
AMERICA, ARRIVING IN THE PACIFIC OCEAN OF
CALIFORNIA, AND SETTLING IN SAN FRANCISCO
WHERE THEY FOUNDED CHINATOWNS, ALONG
THE PACIFIC COAST. IN THAT TRAJECTORY THEY
INTRODUCED NEW FISHING AND FOOD PRACTICES, AS
WELL AS BURIAL AND OTHER BUSINESS TRADITIONS
TO SURVIVE IN THEIR NEW ENVIRONMENT.

CHAPTER 1
In the Beginning …

Chinese genealogy dates back thousands of years. My maternal forebears, the Chows, traced their ancestry to the early 15th century. These ancestors pre-date that time, with a different surname, "Ha," meaning "Summer."

Over a thirty-year period, Lennie Lee made several trips to China, sometimes to research her ancestry and others to visit her grandson Daryl and his family who first lived in Beijing and now in Hong Kong. It was my mother who determined when the Chow Clan began.

On an early visit in the 1970s, Lennie went to her ancestral village to research her genealogy. The trip took place in 1972, before President Richard Nixon visited China.

A photo of Lennie studying the family shrine shows the Clan's initial connections. With help from a couple of guides, she was able to gain information.

L K LENNIE LEE AT THE FAMILY SHRINE

Photo courtesy Roberta Chew.

Accompanied by her niece Roberta, who worked at the United States embassy, Lennie visited her ancestral village of Fou Shack. After her visit to the family shrine, Lennie wrote about the surname Chow.

> *Fou Shack was a village of the comparatively wealthy and powerful Chew family clan of 9,000 people. One of the Chew girls married Ha Jun Gwun, General Ha … more than five hundred years ago … he was my paternal ancestor, and I visited his tombstone and paid respect. When he was a seaman sailing overseas, one of General Ha's sons adopted his mother's name, Chew.*

The inscriptions on the tombstone link General Ha to the early 15th century. Because of his low socioeconomic status, General Ha kept his surname, but later generations chose Chew because it denoted higher status. Thus began the Chew or Chow family lines, which covered the period between 1,368 to 1,644 of the Ming Dynasty. Significant is the mention of a son taking the name Chew; while sailing overseas, he would have been a Ming soldier because they were the only ones sailing overseas. This is likely the beginning of the Chow Clan seafaring tradition.

General Ha Jun Gwun lived near Nanjing during the Ming Dynasty. At first, I thought this was impressive because the Chow Clan began with a military general. However, it was not as glamorous as I thought.

Ha's ancestors were part of a system known as the Hereditary Military. However, being a Ming Dynasty soldier, even a general, did not necessarily express high status. The Hereditary System required sending a family member for service whenever it was demanded. According to Kenneth Swope (2014),

> Hereditary soldiers were meant to be self-sufficient. They provided their own food via military farms (tun tian) and rotated into training and military posts such as the capital, where specialized drilling with firearms was provided. Soldiering was one of the lowest professions in the Ming dynasty. Military officers were not only subordinate to civil officials, but

generals and soldiers alike were degraded, treated with fear, suspicion, and distaste. Military service enjoyed far less prestige than its civil counterpart due to its hereditary status and because most soldiers were illiterate. (*The Military Collapse of China's Ming Dynasty:* London: Routledge, 2014, np).

THE MING DYNASTY

Swope (2014) argued that besides their low economic status, these soldiers resided in Tuntian or Tunken spaces—a type of frontier military-agricultural colony over the history of China. Troops were sent to harsh landscapes at the Chinese frontier to turn uncultivated land into self-sustained, settler colonies. In other words, they doubled as peasant farmers.

Even though the Clan had a lowly status, being part of the Ming Dynasty was initially impressive.

The reigning emperor of the Ming Dynasty in the early 15th century was Yongle (Yong Luh). He was ambitious and created multiple projects. The newly named Chow Clan were hereditary soldiers under his reign. They did not have high status but ended up serving the Ming Dynasty for centuries.

EMPEROR YONGLE, MING DYNASTY, EARLY 15TH CENTURY
Unknown artist.

THE FORBIDDEN CITY

The capital of China was located at Nanjing, when Yongle decided to move his court to Beijing and built a huge palace complex, which became known as the Forbidden City.

It was occupied by twenty-four emperors of the Ming and subsequent Ching Dynasties for more than 500 years. The palace is now open to the public, and millions of people from all over the world visit. It is a UNESCO cultural heritage site.

THE FORBIDDEN CITY—BEIJING, CHINA
Courtesy of Wikimedia.org.

THE GREAT WALL OF CHINA
Courtesy of WikipediaCommons.org.

THE GREAT WALL

Yongle's ambition did not stop with building the new capital. Moving the palace north also meant needing protection from the warring Mongols to the North. China had begun building a wall to keep out neighboring warriors, but Yongle extended the wall over 3,800 miles. With that, he also undertook one of the largest sea explorations ever.

THE MUSLIM ADMIRAL

The greatest Chinese seafarer in history, perhaps ever, was Zheng He (pronounced Zeng huh), who commanded a huge fleet in the 15th century at the behest of Ming Emperor Yongle. Zheng was over seven feet tall with a sixty-inch waist; a Muslim who was captured as a young boy when the Yunnan Province battled and lost to the Ming army. A servant in the Ming court, because of his military prowess and loyalty, Zheng He became a trusted lieutenant of the Ming Emperor Yongle. He ascended to commander of the largest fleet in Chinese history. It featured upwards of sixty-three Treasure Ships that were larger than a football field.

ZHENG HE, SEAFARER
Courtesy of Wikipedia.org.

JUNK OF ZHENG HE

Illustration by Christian Jegou, Science Photo Library.

The above illustration shows a cut-away section of a Treasure Ship with many compartments to hold various objects. The compartments were sealed, which made the vessel, despite its huge size, very seaworthy and not susceptible to sinking. Next to the ship is an example of a support Junk.

A major engineering feat was building an ocean-going Junk that could transport large animals. One gift received was particularly interesting: a giraffe.

A partial replica of one of Zheng He's treasure ships displaying its below-deck cargo is at the Maritime Experiential Museum in Singapore.

A PARTIAL REPLICA OF ONE OF ZHENG HE'S TREASURE SHIPS
Photo by Minyun Zhou, Dreamstime.com.

Support vessels numbered around 250 with a crew of 27,000. From the east coast of China to Africa, Admiral He's flotilla sailed over 100,000 sea miles during seven voyages, with multiple ports of call in between. The voyages were not military operations but instead were meant to exert influence over nations alongside the Indian Ocean. At some ports of call, gift exchanges took place.

During his voyages, Zheng He took time to make a pilgrimage to Mecca and established several Mosques at places he visited. A major disappointment for the fleet was that its voyages, in the end, were all for naught. Zheng died on the sixth voyage. The entire armada was taken apart after the seventh voyage, which transported returning emissaries. The ship's logs were burned in an attempt to erase all records of its travels.

ZING HE'S VISITS TO THE WEST AS DEPICTED IN
"HEAVENLY PRINCESS CLASSICS" (1420)
Courtesy of Wikipedia Commons.

The Ming Dynasty entered a period where they opted to have nothing to do with the outside world. Still, their "Treasure Ships," more than 60 were up to 400 feet long, along with 250 support vessels crewed by 26,0000 soldiers and sailors—this must have been an impressive sight.

Since historical records do not mention any other overseas sailing during the Ming Dynasty, I have concluded that the Chow Clan were part of the fleet, although at a low level. My mother documents that General Ha Jun Gwun's son was a seaman sailing overseas, which was likely the beginning of a seafaring tradition of the family Clan that lasted six centuries.

CHAPTER 2
Coming to America

Not much is known about our forebears' history during the ensuing four centuries after the Treasure Ship voyages. In 1644, the Ming Dynasty was defeated by the Mongols, and Clan members began migrating south to avoid being beheaded. They settled in the coastal area of Guanghai, also known as Kwong Hoy, in the Southeast region of China. They kept their seafaring heritage, engaging in fishing and trading. Also, because of its dense forests of teak trees, wood products were manufactured, and sailing vessels known as Junks were built.

MAP OF KWONG HOY

Courtesy of Wikipedia Commons.

GRANDFATHER TÀI LǍO YE (太姥爷)

How the Chows came to America is a matter of speculation, as Lennie did not write about the subject. However, based on clues in her writings, I've reached some conclusions. Unfortunately, the name of Lennie's great-grandfather is lost to history. The Chinese language has a specific term that describes every relative. The one that means great grandfather is Tài Lǎo Ye, and this is used to name him. From what Lennie writes we can infer that he and his wife traveled to America because she did write that her grandfather, and their son, Chow Tick Kee, were born in San Francisco.

There's no question Tài Lǎo Ye was motivated to leave Kwong Hoy, as the early 19th century was a terrible time. China's economy was in decline. Food shortages were the norm. Natural disasters such as typhoons and earthquakes wreaked havoc. The British were drug dealers and perpetuated the first Opium War.

The war was the result of the fact that there were many more Chinese products that Britain wanted but other western countries had not much to offer in return. It was decided that smuggling opium into China would generate a market by creating countless addicts.

During those times, British gunboats routinely attacked vessels they encountered in the South China seas. Pirates were also a major problem. By the 1800s, multiple pirate fleets prowled the South China Seas, raiding everything from fishing vessels to large cargos. Foremost amongst the greatest pirate in history was Ching Shih, a beautiful woman who commanded a fleet of 1800 Junks and 80,000 pirates.

Most unusual of all, Ching Shih and her second husband maintained a code of ethics that specified the death penalty for those who violated them. Her greatest achievement was survival. She retired after the Ching Dynasty government issued her a pardon and after that lived comfortably, passing away at age of sixty-nine—ancient for a pirate leader.

Lennie didn't indicate whether the Clan encountered the Ching Shih fleet. Ching Shih's Red Flag fleet was just one of many fleets, although the largest of a confederation of six operated in the early 1800s. They were identified by the color of the flag they flew: red, black, blue, white, yellow, and purple.

CHING SHIH (AKA ZHENG YI SAO) IN AN 1836 ILLUSTRATION
Courtesy of Wikimedia Commons.

Pirates and marauders continued to be a major problem even after Ching Shih retired. Tài Lǎo Ye sailed his own Junk to trade along South China. His village manufactured wood products from small utensils to larger items like shrines and coffins. The villagers were shipwrights as well.

The process of visiting ports of call along the South China Sea allowed Tài Lǎo Ye to conclude that the future for those living in the Guangdong region was not good. It is inferred that sometime in the early 1840s, Tài Lǎo Ye made the decision to emigrate to Mi Ji Jian, also known as America. The exact year is unclear.

The forebears were fortunate enough to have the means to migrate because of their seafaring skills. Once the decision was made to leave, sailing to California was relatively simple.

One unusual circumstance was that historians often wrote that the first migrants to Gum San were those seeking gold. The Clan, likely the first to settle in California, was different because they brought their families. They arrived prior to the Gold Rush and there's no mention of whether or not there were other crew members. It's likely there were, but their names are lost to history.

Lennie indicated that her grandfather, Chow Tick Lee, was born in the United States, after the Clan's arrival. Grandmother's name was Chun Yee. They were welcomed at the time because their fishing skills provided seafood and imported unfamiliar foods and other eatables to local inhabitants.

NING YUNG AND SONS

Another arrival by sea was that of Ning Yung, a long-lost uncle. Our family wasn't aware of this person until Lennie wrote about him. The name Ning Yung translates to peaceful sunshine. He sailed to California sometime between 1833 and 1843 to join Tài Lǎo Ye. His wife's name is unknown. According to Lennie, they had two sons, Ning Choie Tane, born in 1843, and Ning Fook Tane born a few years later. Choie and Fook Tane attended missionary schools and spoke English well.

At that time, there were no regulations about migration; it was simply a matter of "hopping off" when they got to California. They initially camped at an area known as India Basin, on the southeast side of the San Francisco peninsula. The area was selected because it was a nice cove with Islais Creek providing a freshwater stream. They were close to the small Spanish enclave known as Yerba Buena.

The commissioned illustration shows the early residents of San Francisco. Though it is unconfirmed, the small vessel being pointed to is perhaps a fishing Junk approaching the large sailing vessel to supply provisions. At about that time, this is an enterprise the Clan would have engaged. Early on, the Bay was their fishing ground, and found a ready market in Yerba Buena village, the Mission, and the Presidio. They also resupplied ships that docked in the Bay, leading an idyllic life.

Collectively, this group of ancestors will be referred to as the Clan.

CHAPTER 3
Ha Liu Chune or "Shrimp Products Village"

Over the decades, the Clan became involved in many enterprises, but upon arrival, fishing was first. Eva Ma and L K Lennie Lee found that the Chinese community, along with establishing saltwater fishing, started shrimping as an important industry for the Clan.

The first arrivals were welcomed, unlike the hostility that later Chinese immigrants would experience. During the Gold Rush era, John Geary, the city's mayor, welcomed the Chinese as "Celestial Men of Commerce." Residents of the small villages were happy to find that the new arrivals were expert fishermen and could help reap an enormous harvest of fish, shrimp, and clams.

CHINESE SHRIMPING VILLAGE AT SOUTHERN FOOT OF RINCON HILL C. 1859.
Painting by Matilda F. Mott, courtesy California Historical Society.

Clan members were the first to establish a small fishing village just south of where the Ferry Building now stands. Others joined them. The exact number is unclear, but they apparently were from the same Kwong Hoy region. This is when fishing became the Clan's first enterprise. They were not alone; it was somewhat of a common thing to do.

Reflecting on the history of shrimping, L K Lennie Lee noted,

> *Ha Liu Chune, Shrimp Products Village, was already a flourishing Chinese Bay Shrimp fishing village before Yerba Buena was renamed San Francisco, prior to the Gold Rush days. Ha Liu Chune was located at Mission Creek, one of the larger Bay water inlets, at the southwest side of San Francisco Bay, a quarter mile south of the Ferry Building. Ha Liu Chine existed until before World War II when a shortage of labor and job opportunities affected the Chinese and other residents. After a few paychecks all the inhabitants moved out of the village. Ha Liu Chune became another Ghost Chinatown.*

> *The old-time Dil Ha Loo, Shrimper men, estimated … fishermen and shrimper men … from San Francisco Bay to the Sacramento River Delta area, once totaled around 5,000.*

> *The old-day Whites called the myriad fishing villages Little Chinas, or China Camps; Ha Liu was once known as one of the Bay's Little Chinas because a group of Chinese fishermen had settled there before Gold was discovered in California. That was when Chinese fishermen took off to the gold fields. By the time they returned to their fishing site some years later, White politicians had passed … laws forbidding Chinese from fishing and shrimping along the California coast and bays.*

CHAPTER 4
Gum San

YERBA BUENA, 1847

Most treatises on Chinese immigration history posit that their migration pattern began with the advent of the 1849 Gold Rush. It made sense. The 1848 census listed the Chinese population at three. The 1849 census was 54, while 1850 it was over 24,000.

In reality, there were immigrants well before 1848. Although it wasn't well documented, the Clan arrived in the early 1840s and likely settled in what was then Yerba Buena. Their numbers alone would have exceeded 3 in 1848. The year 1849 brought incredible change with the discovery of gold. The news spread like wildfire.

VIEW OF SAN FRANCISCO, FORMERLY YERBA BUENA,
IN 1847, BEFORE THE DISCOVERY OF GOLD

Courtesy of Museum of San Francisco.

By 1850, the Gold Rush was on. Immigrants came in droves. It has been estimated that in just two years after the discovery, 26,000 to 30,000 immigrants came from China. Most were from the Guangzhou region. It was actually quicker timewise to travel from there than the Eastern United States. Before the completion of the Transcontinental Railroad, a ship from New York would need to sail around South America to reach San Francisco. The result was that instead of a small fishing village, the area grew overnight to the largest city on the West Coast.

Ning Yung was enterprising and resourceful, and he was an excellent leader for those who wanted to immigrate to an unfamiliar country. One of the main things he did was to form the Kwong Hoy or Guanghai Seamen's Society to service the needs of arrivals from his native village.

Another thing that favored the Nings was that back in their native village they operated a funeral service in their home village and manufactured coffins and shrines. This, plus their ability to sail back and forth to China, meant that in the unfortunate case of a sojourner perishing while in America, Ning and his family made all necessary arrangements for returning the body home. This became a large enterprise, but initially, only the Nings and the Chows specialized in transporting those from Kwong Hoy.

As the Gold Rush waned, thousands congregated there and a Chinatown began to form in San Francisco. Without the means to return to their native land, a huge bachelor society developed. There was a large labor pool. Many ended up working on building the railroads. Some in agriculture, while still others built much of the infrastructure in California. Business enterprises sprung up to provide goods and services to Chinatown residents—a need developed for someone or something to provide cultural logistics.

In China, a social organization called Huigans was created so that arriving sojourners may adapt to the needs of the increasing number of immigrants.

GETTING ORGANIZED

The history of Chinese immigrant arrivals from Southeast China is erroneously associated with sojourners who were purported to have come for the Gold Rush. In the period between 1850 and 1882, this population grew exponentially. There are reports that up to 322,000 entered or re-entered from China during that period.

A burgeoning Chinatown developed around the west side of Portsmouth Square. Sojourners intended to make a fortune and eventually return to their native villages. They were not a monolithic group. There were many subregions in Guangzhou. Each one helped new arrivals with their organizations known as Huigans.

Early arrivals consisted of young men from farming areas who were illiterate. Their families sent them with the expectation that they could earn money to send home. The prospect of becoming rich was there, but that was pretty much a fantasy. Those who made much money were the merchants who facilitated their arrivals and provided supplies. For the sojourners, their needs were met by Huigans based on the family surname, the same dialect, and the region from where they came. Although Huigans went a long way in facilitating the needs of sojourners, their efforts were not entirely altruistic. For instance, the Huigans instituted a Credit Ticket system, which was essentially a loan to pay for passage. The interest rates ranged from four to eight percent, per month. By agreement, unless they had a release from the Huigan, shipping companies would not allow a sojourner to board without return passage.

Since the Clan arrived before 1849, and because they were far more independent than sojourners, they had no need for a Huigan. However, as the years went by, they formed an organization called the Kwong Hoy Seamen's Society, which helped arrivals from their native village. They provided similar services for Kwong Hoy sojourners at less cost. They founded and provided an important service.

The Clan did not opt to join the Gold Rush. They had wives and children to consider before leaving for the gold fields. They remained fishermen but also recognized that an enterprise they had engaged in back in Kwong Hoy would also be needed in California, what they called Gum San, meaning Gold Mountain. This enterprise was called Jub Gwuck, which in translation means pick up bones.

CHAPTER 5
Jub Gwuck

The discovery of Gold in 1849 brought changes that the Chows and Nings enjoyed. Tens of thousands of Chinese immigrants arrived to seek their fortunes. Historians estimate that between 25,000 and 30,000 people arrived to California between 1849 and 1851. A budding Chinatown developed around the west side of Portsmouth Square. (Wikipidia.org, History of China, February 13, 2023.)

Unfortunately, Gum San or Gold Mountain was a hostile environment fraught with danger. Most sojourners who came did not find a fortune. Many came as indentured servants, thinking they would work in fields or construction for a while, fulfill their obligation, and then seek a fortune or at least send money home to support their families.

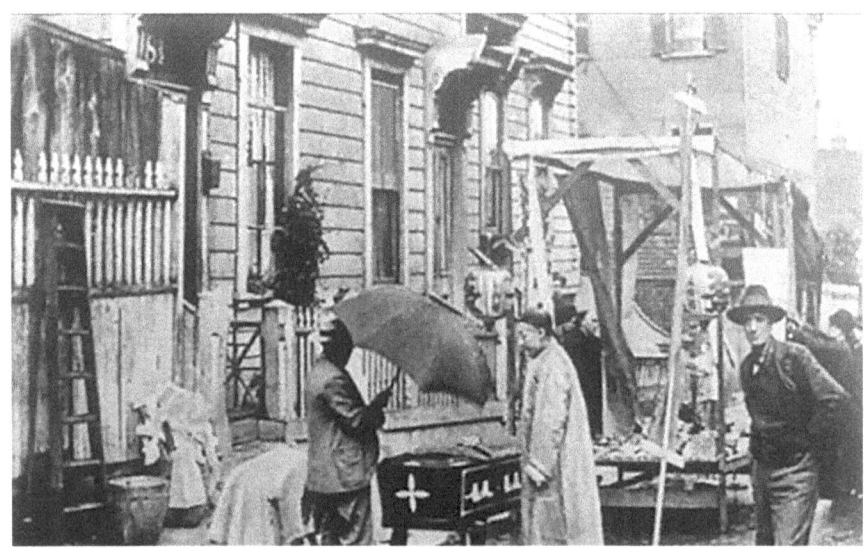

PHOTO BY LOUIS J. STELLMAN, GIFTED TO R.H. DILLON, 1960.
Published in R. H. Dillon, 1976:63.

Xenophobia revealed its ugly sides, and, along with the inevitably declining economic conditions and job competition, many died without ever fulfilling their dreams. Nevertheless, returning remains to the homeland was a sacred custom. Most sojourners were affiliated with associations that facilitated burials, but an issue remained. While some bodies were sent back immediately, more likely it took as much as ten years before the remains were exhumed and shipped home.

The process was known as Jup Gwuck in Chinese, or pick up bones. This was when Ning Yung saw an opportunity to fulfill a need. For those from Kwong Hoy, who died while living in San Francisco, especially the seamen, the Nings sent remains back to China, without going through the expensive process of being sent to Hong Kong.

The Nings back in Kwong Hoy performed funeral ceremonies and were expert woodworkers. They were shipwrights and built beautiful teak wood coffins. A new need arose for boxes and coffins to be sent to America. Ning Yung's sons, Ning Choie Tane and Ning Fook Tane, responded to this demand. Burial preparations were made up to ten years before the remains were exhumed. Markers listed the information needed to send the remains. Chow Chong, born in 1865, eventually worked for the business. The enterprise lasted decades.

ON NOB HILL

During the first two decades of operation, the Ning Yung Cemetery was on some of the most significant real estate in San Francisco's history. For public health and economic reasons, a holding cemetery was established. Yung found an unusual and interesting place—tranquil Huntington Park—that sits serenely at the top of what is now known as Nob Hill. California, Mason, Taylor, and Sacramento Streets bounded the park. Today, world hotels, luxury apartments, great restaurants, and the Tony Pacific Union Club fringe the park. The scene was thought to be somewhat exclusive but does not compare to the site's previous history.

Nob Hill had an entirely different past in the 1850s and '60s, and in the '70s. Some of California's wealthiest residents built ostentatious homes known in what was then called California Hill. It eventually became Nabob Hill because of its haughty residents, until the name was shortened to Nob Hill.

In the mid-1930s, Ning Choie Tane, then in his 80s, often baby-sat Lennie, along with brother George. Mother Ning Shee was busy doing piecemeal work for sewing factories or shelling shrimp for fishermen. One day, they left their dwelling at Dupont, now Grant Avenue and Clay Street and trudged up Clay Street—it was a steep climb. From the base of the hill at Montgomery Street, it was 376 feet to the top. As they approached the high point, they turned left onto a small street called Sproule. Sacramento Street was one block over, and in front of them was tranquil Huntington Park.

The youngsters and their uncle walked back down the hill and did not give it further thought. Lennie never forgot 1203 Sacramento Street.

She would later write,

> *Uncle Choie pointed to the right, where a huge construction project was going on. … This would become*

HUNTINGTON PARK TODAY
Courtesy of Wikimedia Commons.

the iconic Episcopalian Church, Grace Cathedral. He told them that their granduncle, Ning Yung, operated a funeral parlor at the corner of Sacramento and Taylor Streets. The address was 1203 Sacramento. With buildings surrounding the park, the area was fully developed.

Also, Lennie recalled:

The Nings built a wooden shack; to house the carved teakwood altar table they'd brought from China, and for folks to worship during funeral rituals. The shack also served as a funeral parlor. They slept under the altar table at night for several months, then added a prefabricated funeral parlor made in China. Three years later, they added two more prefabricated rooms, a bedroom, and a kitchen. The wooden shack became the storage room for their teakwood coffins and other supplies. They also reserved an area at the northwest side of the cemetery to bury the bones that were expected to be reburied in China. For two decades, the Ning father and sons were the early Chinese cemetery directors, undertakers, and gravediggers.

Then, in 1868, San Francisco passed an ordinance that barred burials anywhere in the city except for land designated in the Northwest corner. This effectively put an end to the Ning Yung Cemetery, and the Nings dug up all the remains and transported them to the City Cemetery, which was located at what is today the Lincoln Park Golf Course. The burial site was vacated at a loss. Nob Hill later became the site of some of history's largest, most lavish homes.

THE CROCKER SPITE FENCE

Charles Crocker, industrialist and banker, wanted to purchase 1203 Sacramento to complete the acquisition of the whole block to build his mansion. When the owner refused, Crocker built a forty-foot-high spite fence that surrounded the property.

A bit of a mystery must be noted. The owner of the Sacramento Street house was listed as someone named Nicholas Yung, not Ning Yung. Nicholas Yung was a German immigrant who listed himself as a cemetery worker. Chinese immigrants were not allowed to own property. Did Ning Yung and Nicholas Yung have some sort of a business relationship? This was irrelevant to the Clan descendants, since there was no claim for the property. It's interesting to wonder about it.

MUYBRIDGE SF PAN 1878 PORTION SHOWING SPITE FENCE
Courtesy of Wikimedia Commons.

CHAPTER 6
The Mystery of China Beach

The Northwest corner of San Francisco has one of the most scenic beaches in California, if not the world, because of China Beach. How this lovely place got that name is a mystery.

On its website, the National Parks Service (NPS) describes this peaceful, beautiful place:

> China Beach, a small, sandy cove between Lands' End and Baker Beach in San Francisco's Sea Cliff neighborhood is used today as a public recreation area that offers spectacular views of the Marina. It was once used as a camp for Chinese fishermen who in the 1800s may have anchored their boats in the harbor.
>
> The State of California bought the beach in 1933 and officially named it James D. Phelan Memorial Beach State

CHINA BEACH
Courtesy of Wikimedia Commons.

Park after the 25th mayor of San Francisco. In 1974, the state turned the beach over to the National Park Service, which recommended changing the name back to China Beach. (National Parks Service, NPS np.)

California bought the beach from a private party with a $50,000 dollar donation from the James D. Phelan estate, so naming the beach after him made sense. Phelan would have been annoyed at the previous name, China Beach.

The 25th mayor of San Francisco was one of the most ardent supporters of the Chinese Exclusion Acts of 1882 and 1892. In 1901, Phelan wrote a vitriolic piece entitled "Why the Chinese should be Excluded" excoriating Chinese and Japanese Americans. After acquiring the property, the NPS showed much wisdom in reverting to its original name. Thus, a privately donated monument was erected in 1982, and still stands at the entrance of the beach.

The inscription on the monument provided by the Chans reads,

> Since the Gold Rush, this cove has been a campsite for many of the Chinese fishermen who worked in and around San Francisco Bay. Their efforts to supply the needs of a young city helped establish one of the area's most important industries and traditions (See National Park Service, npa.org).

CHINA BEACH WITH GOLDEN GATE BRIDGE

Courtesy of Wikimedia Commons.

Still, a question remains about whether China Beach is an appropriate name. The well-meaning but perhaps not so well-informed Chinese family that donated the monument suggests the misleading idea that Chinese fishermen used the cove and were valued members of San Francisco's history when neither was the case.

Even the NPS had its doubts. Its websites states that, "There is little evidence of Chinese habitation at the Cove...," inferring misleading notions that Chinese fishermen used the cove and were valued members of San Francisco's history "when neither was the case" (National Park Service, nps.org).

City and state politicians attempted to eliminate the Chinese fishery. This is not meant to disparage the donors who founded a successful chain of restaurants, as their intent was to celebrate the successes of Chinese immigrants. The problem is that visitors who view the monument get a distorted view of the area's history. In reality, politicians actively barred Chinese from fishing. In regard to this conflict, the National Park Service explains:

> In 1860, two discriminatory laws were passed in California. One forbade Chinese American children from attending public schools. The other required Chinese American fishermen to purchase a special permit. It was called a license because unequal taxation was forbidden by law, and to tax Chinese fishermen and not Italian or Portuguese would have been illegal. The NPS provided a distorted view of the history of China Beach.

> The Foreign Miners Tax of 1850 forced Chinese out of the goldfields, and they returned to the San Francisco Bay to become fishermen. Their main catch was shrimp, but they also took sturgeon, smelt, herring, abalone, and crab. By 1875, there "were 25 Chinese shrimp camps along the shores of San Francisco Bay" (National Park Service, nps.org).

It is not known how these men used China Beach but it is clear that it would have been a poor shrimp camp, as the foggy weather made it difficult for the shrimp to dry. Outside the Golden Gate, the beach may have been an abalone gathering or safe landing spot (National Park Service, nps.org).

In the 1880s, Chinese made up 50 percent of all fishing crews in the San Francisco Bay Area. Threatened by their success and acting to force Chinese rivals out of the industry, fisherman relied on anti-Chinese laws and discriminatory tactics. By the 1890s, only 20 percent of Bay fishers were Chinese, and the number continued to decrease through the rest of the century (National Park Service, nps.org).

In 1880, the State Legislature first enacted a law prohibiting *Aliens* from fishing in the Bay and beyond. However, they soon came to terms that many, if not most of the Italian, Portuguese, and Irish fishermen were non-native aliens.

Chinese ethnics did not react passively. They were adept at using the legal system to fight for their rights and quickly pointed out that the law violated the 14th Amendment. The ordinance was quickly rewritten to bar fishing by anyone who had a queue—a Chinese hairstyle for men—which was common among them. Eventually, all fishing rights for Chinese were barred, starting at the Ferry building on the east side of the city and going out to the Pacific Ocean. This, of course, would have included China Beach. Because they were not part of the White people's diet, fishing for shrimp and other shellfish like abalone was allowed. As a result, numerous China Camps were allowed to exist as grassy fishing areas where the crustaceans could be found were not so desirable.

The Southeast area of San Francisco, now known as Hunter's Point or the North Bay area, there is a China Camp still in existence in Marin County. Even though the China Beach monument inscription states that fishing is one of the area's most important industries and traditions, one would be hard-pressed to find evidence for the presence of Chinese fishermen.

Today, Fisherman's Wharf, located in North Beach, is one of San Francisco's most famous attractions. It is largely an appropriate celebration of Italian American heritage, but there is minimal evidence of Chinese immigrants.

A significant description as to why there was limited fishing by Chinese comes from a biography written by Jack London. His novels are some of the most iconic in literary history. The city of Oakland named an important area of the city Jack London Square. The state memorialized him with Jack London State Historic Park in Glen Ellen. He is deserving of all the accolades he has received, but there is an unfortunate story that remains buried. As a young man, Jack London was part of the Fish Patrol—an armed posse that boarded fishing vessels in the San Francisco Bay for alleged violation of laws passed ostensibly to protect the Bay fishery. Unfortunately, many of the ordinances barred Chinese Fishermen. London is revered in literary circles, but for Chinese people, his work on the Fish Patrol was an unfortunate part of his legacy. He wrote about their lives as if these were his experiences.

The Fish Patrol was an armed posse that boarded fishing vessels in the San Francisco Bay for alleged violation. In this regard, historian Eve Armentrout-Ma wrote (Jan 1, 1981).

> The San Francisco area was the northern limit of these fishermen. Oral tradition holds that they had an anchorage at Phelan Beach—once popularly known as China Beach. ... Fishermen lit large bonfires at

COVER OF JACK LONDON'S *TALES OF THE FISH PATROL*
Courtesy of Project Gutenburg.

night on the beaches, exciting much comment from shore observers, who thought … they were pirates. (1981, np, out of print.)

In addition to abalone, Chinese fishermen off of the Golden Gate National Recreation Area (GGNR) territory caught fish. "Some of it was caught by fishermen on ocean-going Junks. These Junks had shore headquarters from San Diego up the coast to near San Simeon" (Ma, 1981, np, out of print).

Thus, the area was not a base for fishing. Rather, as the National Park Service stated, the cove was a "safe landing spot just outside the Golden Gate." Using the cove as an anchorage would be useful for a non-fishing enterprise. During the latter half of the 19th century, locals often saw Chinese Junks, including Ning Yung's, anchored in the cove. It was assumed that these were fishermen, but they were there for a different reason: the presence of a Golden Gate Cemetery.

In 1868, the land where the Legion of Honor and Lincoln Park Golf Course sit today was reserved by the city for Golden Gate Cemetery. The first interment took place in July 1870. Evicted from their Nob Hill location, they were there to move the remains in their holding cemetery to the new site. For their family, this was an opportunity but it needed to be done in secret.

Lennie recalled that these societies were linked across the ocean. She explained,

> *San Francisco's Kwong Hoy Seamen Society, a sub-chapter of the Chinese Seamen Society of China, was said to have established the first Chinese seamen holding cemetery in San Francisco. Granduncle Choie Tane, my father, and other Root Old-timer fishermen claimed that subsequently, several other Chinese holding cemeteries were established on the West Coast long before 1850, even more than a hundred years before the discovery of gold in California. Holding cemeteries are temporary sites where the bodies of the deceased were later dug up to be sent back to China.*
>
> *Because … the Kwong Hoy seamen wanted their bodies sent back to China, if they should die in America, the*

Kwong Hoy Society Cemetery served as the holding cemetery until the next Chinese Junk ship was on its way back to China. Then it would be time to Jub Gwuck and rebury them among loved ones.

Today, that site is the location of the Legion of Honor Museum and Lincoln Park golf course. The new cemetery was close to China Beach, making it easier to load remains for return to China.

Crossing town by horse and cart or on the Ferries and Cliffhouse Railway, as shown on the map, would have been extremely dangerous for Chinese people because White laborers worked on nearby projects. Ning Yung, his two sons, and workers, and possibly a German immigrant using the alias Nicholas Yung, exhumed the bodies being held in the Nob Hill holding cemetery and moved the remains to the new cemetery.

In her account, Lennie wrote an explanation of the 150-year-old mystery of how the cove got its name. She explained,

The northwest side of San Francisco facing the Pacific Ocean was selected for the cemetery because of its hilly terrain along the ocean beach and because of the isolated, serene environment surrounded by colorful flowers, thriving greenery, and shade trees where one could be

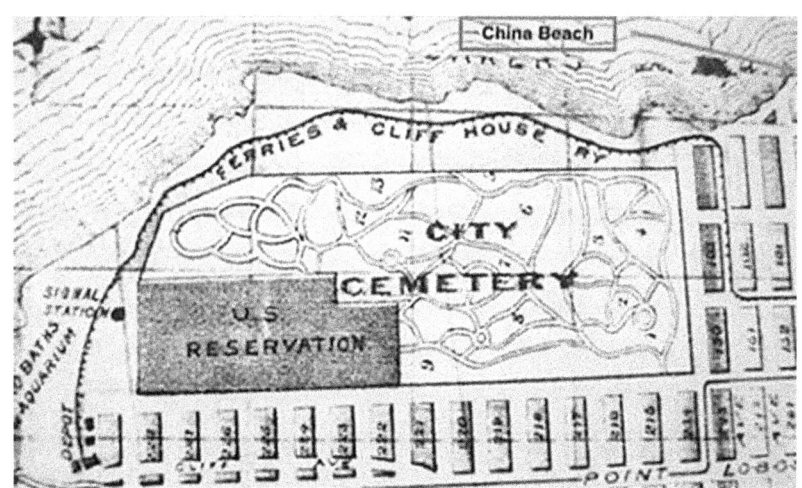

KWONG HOY SOCIETY CEMETERY
Courtesy of www.frederickbee.com/ahyute.html.

buried in peace. The Fown-Shan-Shui and Wind-
Mountain-Water provided peaceful, quiescent, and
tranquil surroundings for ... seamen who died.

The seamen anchored their Chinese Junk ships around
the China Beach area near the Sea Cliff, now part of
the Golden Gate National Recreation Area (GGNRA).
Fishing was poor, and they left. Meanwhile, the Ning
family quietly Jub Gwuck bodies from the Kwong Hoy
Seamen Society Cemetery under the moonlight and re-
turned them to China.

China Beach marks a historical space whereby many sojourners with high hopes came to Gum San. However, what they found was disappointment and death. They were fortunate to return to their homeland as custom dictated. Eve Armentrout-Ma (1972) recorded that Junks anchoring at the cove might've been collecting abalone, while they tended to the needs of the dead. Abalone was a valuable commodity, not only for the flesh but for the shells—mother of pearl used to make jewelry. Because of overfishing, abalone soon disappeared. As for the departed, their last stop in America would have been China Beach.

SUNSET AT CHINA BEACH
Painting by Elaine Presser, courtesy of Mike Gaughan.

PART II

THE MAVERICK

CHOW CHONG IS MY MATERNAL
GRANDFATHER. THUS, I CONFESS A BIT OF
BIAS WHEN I STATE HE WAS ONE OF THE
MOST INCREDIBLE JOKE SINGS. HIS STORY
IS THE STUFF OF LEGENDS.

CHAPTER 7
Chow Chong

Chow Chong was a scofflaw, bootlegger, smuggler, convict, and all-around roustabout. Ironically, for anyone of Chinese descent who dared to roam outside Chinatowns as he did, these attributes were necessary to survive.

Chong's Father, Chow Tick Kee, was born near Yerba Buena in 1833. Likely he was one of the first-ever Chinese persons born in the United States. Lennie didn't offer details about Chong's mother, Chun Yee, except for her bound feet. It would have been interesting to know about her, since Afong May is generally acknowledged as the first Chinese woman who came to America, but Chun Lee preceded her by at least one year. They only had one child.

As a young boy, Chow's regular hangout was Portsmouth Square, open space located on the eastern edge of Chinatown. It was an oasis for San Franciscans of all stripes and popular for residents of Chinatown. It remains so to this day.

CHOW CHONG IN 1897 & 1904
Family archives.

The family lived at 620 Dupont Street, later named Grant Avenue, where his father operated a small business manufacturing cigar boxes for the hundreds of small cigar-making operations throughout Chinatown. Tick Kee also sailed back and forth with the family to Kwong Hoy, which took place every seven to ten years.

Chong worked for his father at a very young age, delivering cigar boxes throughout Chinatown. When thinking about what enterprises Chinese operated, laundries are the first business that come to mind, but several thousand residents of Chinatown could have been found manufacturing cigars. This type of business was easily set up and took relatively little space and equipment. Other enterprises included boot and shoe making, and clothing.

Beginning in the early 1800s, the one square block area fronting San Francisco Bay, which was then at Montgomery Street, was a traditional plaza named Plaza de Yerba Buena. The area was Mexican territory. After it was taken over by the United States in 1848 with the signing of the Treaty of Guadalupe Hidalgo, it

ARNOLD GENTHE'S PHOTOGRAPH OF YOUNG CHILDREN
AT PORTSMOUTH SQUARE
Courtesy of Wikipedia Commons.

became Portsmouth Plaza, then Portsmouth Square. The Square was teeming with Chinese people.

Lennie provided a brief description and history of the Square. She shared,

> One day, while we stood looking out the second-story hallway window of the Suey Ying Tong Headquarters overlooking Portsmouth Square, Granduncle Choie Tane told us the story of why Portsmouth Square, in the middle of Chinatown, was named the Harbor's Mouth, when the little park was two miles inland from the harbor. Granduncle Choie Tane also clarified why Chinatown folks called our segregated neighborhood Tong Yung Fou, Tang People Port, instead of translating the basic meaning of Chinatown into Chinese.
>
> The term Chinatown came about when White racists sought to encamp all Chinese within the twelve square blocks around Portsmouth Square. Chinatown was a segregationist term coined by Yellow Journalism media. The Chinatown folks with racial and heritage pride named their segregated neighborhood

PORTSMOUTH SQUARE
Courtesy of Wikipedia Commons.

*Tong Yun Fou, Tang People Port, in memory of China's Tong
Chiu, Tang Dynasty (618-907).*

*China was powerful then, and Chinese were respected as a
people. They called their Chinatown language Tong Yun Hwa,
Tang People Language, Chinese Language; their main street,
Sacramento Street, Tong Yun Gai, Tang People Street; their
style of cooking Tong Choun, Tang Meals, Chinese Meals; their
homeland Tong Saun, Tang Mountains, China; their Chinese
schools Tong Yun She Goon, Tang People Schools, and themselves Tong Yun, Tang People, Chinese.*

*Cities in California also have economic and cultural unification
names that were not phonetically translated, such as: Second
Port, Sacramento; Sam Fou, Third Port, Stockton. Chinese
gold miners named the hills and mountains of California
they'd mined, such as Kim Shan, Gold Mountains, and old
gold-mining towns, such as Weaverville, Kim Shan Sing, Gold
Mountains Town.*

Residents of Chinatown were proud of their culture and re-
named streets and towns to make them their own. Invested in
their community, Chinese were a hard-working people. As such,
childhood was brief for many of the children. They were assigned
domestic work to earn money early in life. When Chong was eight
or nine years old, he began delivering cigar boxes manufactured by
his father.

As Chong grew up, Lennie described him as an adventurous
young man.

> *Chow Chong was known to be somewhat of a bilin-
> gual maverick and roustabout during his younger days.
> As one of the original Joke Sings, he loved eating hom
> yue fon—salted fish with rice—and roast prime rib with
> mashed potatoes and gravy. As a child, he wanted to cut
> his queue and wear Western-style clothing.*

His parents refused but allowed him to dress in Western style. It was still the Ching Dynasty, and cutting his queue would affect his parents' business of selling dried shrimps, scallops, abalone, salted fish, tree seeds, and seedlings to China.

The Chows would get into a lot of trouble or might even be beheaded by the imperial Mandarins, if they should sail back to China without their queues. So, he waited until his parents retired back to China during the 1890s and then cut it. He also had a number of White friends with whom he drank and socialized in the Barbary Coast Bowery.

One of those friends was legendary author Robert Louis Stevenson. Their short friendship is the stuff of legends and one that only appropriated Chinese experiences.

CHAPTER 8
Robert Louis Stevenson or "RLS"

Famed author Robert Louis Stevenson (RLS) was not someone that would associate with Chinese Americans, let alone be a family friend to the Clan. They briefly knew each other, but the influence the Clan had on Stevenson evidenced quite a story.

It was the year 1879, when RLS endeavored to convince his lover, Fanny Osbourne, to divorce her philandering husband and marry him. At the time, she was living in Monterey, California. To be near her, RLS traveled there from Scotland. He was not yet a successful author but was keen on experiencing lifestyles other than the one of privilege with his well-to-do family. He decided to travel as an *Amateur Emigrant* to see what it was like to land in America, then go by Railroad from New York to Monterey. His three works: *The Amateur Emigrant, Across the Plains,* and *The Silverado Squatters* (1892) reflect that experience. When Fanny decided to leave her husband, Stevenson moved to San Francisco to await final divorce proceedings.

ROBERT LOUIS STEVENSON
Courtesy of Wikipedia Commons.

In San Francisco, at 608 Bush Street, he lived a spartan life, mainly exploring the area around him, taking notes and writing short stories about his encounters. His desire to experience life as an emigre was a metaphor for the changes, he sought from the gentleman's life he had in Scotland.

His choice of living location was an interesting one—it put him in the middle of many things going on in San Francisco in 1880. His place of residence gave him a good vantage point for his writing. To the southwest, a labor movement called the Workingman's Party of California was agitating for the elimination of Chinese workers perceived as unfairly taking jobs away. To the northwest was the top of Nob Hill, where *Robber Barons* had built gigantic, ostentatious homes to display their wealth. RLS called it the *Hill of Palaces*. To the northeast was Chinatown, and a little bit further, the raucous Barbary Coast. Along the way, there was a walking place designed to foster compassion and understanding through theatrical experiences.

RLS AND THE CHINESE

RLS's first mention of encounters with Chinese people appears to have been in August of 1879, as he crossed the country on Transcontinental Railroad. Later in *Across the Plains,* he remarked that he was impressed with the cleanliness and organization of his fellow Chinese travelers. In *The Despised Race*, he shows his disdain for the attitudes Whites held toward Chinese. He wrote,

> A while ago, it was the Irish, and now the Chinese must go. Such is the cry. It seems, after all, that no country is bound to submit to immigration any more than to invasion; each is a war to the knife and resistance to either but legitimate defense. Yet we may regret the free tradition of the republic, which loved to depict herself with open arms, welcoming all unfortunates. And certainly, as a man who believes that he loves freedom, I may be excused some bitterness when I find her sacred name misused in the contention (1892, pp. 19-20).

Robert Louis Stevenson wrote *Across the Plains* while living in San Francisco. Part of Stevenson's daily routine was to visit Portsmouth Square.

In 1880, people likely did not pay much notice to the gaunt, emaciated man with a constant cough who frequently came to sit and people watch. He dressed shabbily and spoke with an unusual accent, a Scottish brogue, but was friendly when approached. He was an aficionado of the Bohemian lifestyle, which partially explained the way he looked. Young children were drawn to him because he was an excellent storyteller, and groups of young children often gathered around him as he told wild tales.

Also living and working nearby were the Nings, Chow Chong's great-granduncle Ning Yung and granduncles Ning Choie Tane and Ning Fook Tane. Their homes and freight forwarding business directly faced Portsmouth Square.

Chow Chong, who was a teenager at the time, met Stevenson in the square and in a twist, regaled the writer with tales of his family's seafaring adventures. The Clan befriended RLS and even took him around to see nearby sights, including the infamous Barbary Coast. Although Stevenson was sickly, he enjoyed the bawdy scenes and wrote about them.

During this era, hatred for the Chinese was rampant. Riots and murders were routine. Stevenson's empathy was highly unusual. A character in *Warrior* named Dylan Leary was patterned after a vicious racist named Denis Kearney. Ironically, Stevenson had an interesting view of him.

DENIS THE MENACE

Stevenson (1979) wrote,

> It was but the other day that I heard a vulgar fellow in the Sandlot, the popular tribune of San Francisco, roaring for arms and butchery. At the call of Abraham Lincoln, said the orator, "ye rose in the name of freedom to set free the negroes; can ye not rise and liberate yourselves from a few dirty

Mongolians?" (*The Haunts of Robert Louis Stevenson*, October 20, 1979, np).

He later made a reference to rabble-rouser, Denis Kearney. Unlike the mischievous cartoon and television character Dennis the Menace, Kearney was an extreme xenophobe and racist. While staying at 608 Bush Street, RLS noted much commotion going on in City politics with the Workingman's Party of California. It took place near City Hall. RLS routinely had meals at a nearby inexpensive restaurant and would listen in from-time-to-time. He showed open contempt for the likes of Kearny, a sentiment shared by historians.

There are those who temper the Kearney image, arguing that *Robber Baron* capitalists of the time—those who exploited workers of all races—were his target. Unfortunately, Kearney attacked Chinese workers when tackling industrialists like Charles Crocker, who hired Chinese workers to build the railroads.

DENIS KEARNEY
Courtesy of Wikipedia Commons.

WONG CHIN FOO

He was a badass journalist and activist of the Exclusion Era. Chin Foo was an opponent of Kearney.

Credited with coning the term Chinese American, Wong Chin Foo was known for following Kearney wherever he went and challenged him on his views. When Wong Chin Foo finally debated Kearney, newspaper reports identified Wong Chin Foo the winner.

At one point, Wong Chin Foo challenged Kearney to a duel, but the Irishman played coy. Apparently, Kearney was a bit of a wimp. In 1873, Wong Chin Foo applied for and was granted U.S. citizenship. He passed away while in China and died a Joke Sing.

When they wrote their respective stories, Bruce and Grandma Lee had action-packed adventure stories in mind. It should be noted that the eastern boundary of Chinatown is Kearny Street, which is named after Stephen W. Kearny, an early military governor of California.

RLS wrote about his encounters with Chinese, and showed great empathy, not only for them, but also for Native Americans.

WONG CHIN FOO
Courtesy of Wikipedia Commons.

Scholars have chronicled RLS's life in great detail. However not much has been written about his thoughts and interactions with sojourners and Joke Sings or members of other ethnic groups. When thinking about the Indian question, RLS wrote,

> Another race shared among my fellow passengers in the disfavor of the Chinese, and that, it is hardly necessary to say, was the noble red man of an old story—over whose own hereditary continent we had been steaming all these days. I saw no wild or independent Indian; indeed, I hear that such avoid the neighborhood of the train, but now and again at way stations, a husband and wife and a few children, disgracefully dressed out with the sweepings of civilization, came forth and stared upon the emigrants.

> The silent stoicism of their conduct and the pathetic degradation of their appearance would have touched any thinking creature. Still, my fellow passengers danced and jested around them with a truly Cockney baseness. I was ashamed of the thing we call civilization. We should carry upon our consciences so much, at least, of our forefathers' misconduct as we continue to profit by ourselves.

> In *Across the Plains*, Robert Louis Stevenson wrote, "Indeed, the Chinese fishermen were so successful that serious conflict developed with Italian American fishermen who began to work the waters of Monterey Bay in the late 1800s." This conflict further contributed to tensions and prejudices against Monterey's Chinese fishing community, and RLS wondered whether Jim Hawkins was the Chinese narrator and main character in *Treasure Island* (Kemp et al. 1995-2005).

As she looked back at those times, L K Lennie Lee documented the ways in which conflict arose in the Monterey Bay Area. She detailed,

My Father, Chow Chong, told us that Kwong Hoy Bay, facing the South China Seas, and Monterey Bay, facing the Pacific Ocean, were both half-moons shaped with similar lowland beaches and sea cliffs several hundred feet above sea level, which ... were outlooks for incoming pirate ships. Monterey Bay's outlook was said to be at the cliffs of China Point, Pacific Grove. On clear sunny days, homesick Kwong Hoy seamen climbed up on top of the peak and claimed they could see the sea cliffs, the China Points of Kwong Hoy Bay, thousands of miles away.

RLS described the protagonist as an intrepid young teenager who faced many challenges but grew to meet them all. In 1881, RLS started writing *Treasure Island* as a serial in "Young Folks," a popular children's magazine, under the title "The Sea Cook." Eventually, it was published as a novel in 1883. It was hugely successful and it brought RLS from near poverty to wealth. The timing of his writings coincides with the outgoing, adventurous, and very Americanized Chow Chong who was his friend. Besides regaling each other, children gathered at Portsmouth Square with adventure stories. Lennie recalled Chong, as a strapping young man—it is thought that uncles Ning Fook Tane and Ning Choie Tane took RLS to the Bella Union Theater, which faced the Square and to the Barbary Coast; in those days it was a den of iniquity.

Stevenson wouldn't have gone there himself. Young Chong would have had one of his many uncles accompany them for security. Being *Shanghaied* or kidnapped was a common occurrence in those days. Routinely ships short on crews drugged sailors while they were at one of the bars or brothels and took them unconscious aboard vessels. Upon awakening, the poor soul would find himself out to sea and was forced to become a crew member. Stevenson was a gaunt, sickly man and going there alone would have been out of the question. Chong was known there and even worked as a bouncer when he was a bit older.

In short, Stevenson would have relied on the image of his young friend, Chow. On the other hand, he stayed in San Francisco out of decorum. He had become engaged to Fanny Osbourne, which would have been foremost in his mind. Obviously, and, in particular, because of the passage of the 1882 Chinese Exclusion Act, a Chinese protagonist would have been out of the question.

When Stevenson told the Clan he wanted to go to Monterey, it turned out that the Nings routinely sailed there. Fook Tane was a fisherman who caught shrimp and other shellfish. He regularly sailed down the coast to Pacific Grove, where there was a large Chinese fishing village to bring such items as kitchen utensils to trade for dried squid. He would then sail with a boatload of the product back to China, where it was popular foodstuff. On the return trip, Fook Tane transported teakwood coffins built by woodworkers in his native village.

Sometime between January and March 1880, Fook Tane, along with a young Chow Chong, took RLS to Pacific Grove. Years later, Lennie retold the sailing story she had gathered through an oral history with Soon Lee, a crew member on the Ning Fook Tane Junk.

In 1931, Lennie went on her first trip outside of Chinatown to the shrimping village of Ha Liu Chune with members of the family and her brother George. There, she met someone who confirmed the Stevenson story. Lennie recalled the guided tour.

George decided to give me a guided tour, a young teenager named Sun Was, whom George had met at the Chinatown YMCA on Sacramento Street, joined us. Sun introduced us to his grandfather, Soon Lee... who said he once worked for Ning Fook Tane. She recalled his words.

"My first job in the United States was as a Dil Ha Loya shrimper man for your relative Ning Fook Tane. I sailed up and down the California coast with him ... for more than ten years. I also met Robert Louis Stevenson, the writer; he rode on our Chinese Junk ships to Monterey Bay a couple of times."

In his writings, RLS wrote a depiction that clearly reflects the Chinese village.

The boats that ride in the haven are of strange and outlandish design; if you walk into the hamlet, you behold costumes and faces that are unfamiliar to the memory. The joss sticks or incense burns, the opium pipe is smoked; the floors are strewn with strips of colored paper—prayers, you would say that somehow missed their destination—and a man guiding his upright pencil from right to left across the sheet, writes home the news of Monterey to the Celestial Empire (Stevenson, November 1880, pp. 647-657).

Jonathan Kemp of The Monterey County Historical Society also described a scene that was impressive.

Those early days of Cannery Row was the arrival of large, ocean-going Chinese Junks with their massive lanteen sails. These splendid craft would anchor off China Point, where they would unload Oriental goods for the local Chinese, then load their holds with dried squid—a food staple and fertilizer much sought after in China. (Monterey County Historical Society, "Chinese Start Monterey Fishing Industry, 1995-2005," (https://bit.ly/4jrF01k).

CHOW CHONG AND SKELETON ISLAND
In her journal, Lennie digs deeply into burial and returns of the deceased. She wrote about the culture and its practices.

Some of the Kwong Hoy seamen wanted their bodies sent back to China if they should die in America, and therefore, the Kwong Hoy Society Cemetery in San

Francisco was established as the holding cemetery until the next Chinese Junk ship was on its way back to China; then it was time to Jub Gwuck and rebury them among loved ones. The northwest side of San Francisco facing the Pacific Ocean was selected for the cemetery because of its hilly terrain along the ocean beach and because of the isolated, serene environment surrounded by colorful flowers, thriving greenery, and shade trees where one could be buried in peace. The Fown-Shan-Shui, Wind-Mountain-Water, provided peaceful, quiescent, and tranquil surroundings for the homesick seamen who died.

Skeleton Island was described as having a dense forest, which China Beach had on its cliff. The high point above the beach could have been Spyglass Hill.

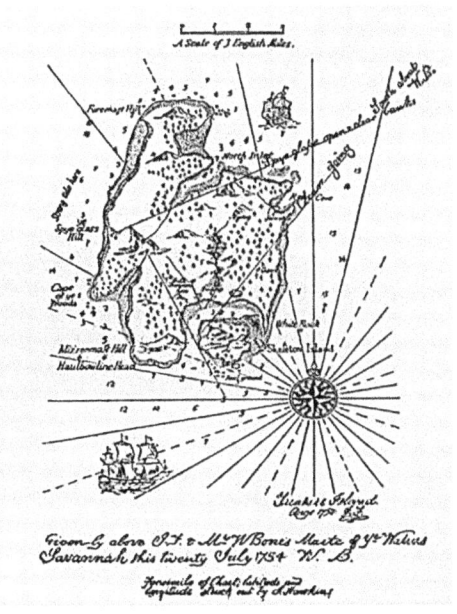

SKELETON ISLAND
Courtesy of Wikipedia Commons.

The friendship between the Nings, Chow Chong, and RLS was brief. Stevenson went on to marry Fanny Osbourne in May of 1880 and lived in California's wine country. Although penniless at the time, with the publication of *Treasure Island*, Stevenson's fortunes improved, and he was recognized as one of the great writers in history.

Stevenson didn't fully benefit from the craze he'd created since copyright laws failed to prevent an unauthorized Samoa publication—this tropical getaway that appeared to promise relaxation.

During his Samoan period, Stevenson led as colorful a life as any of his novels. RLS became involved in local politics, campaigning for Samoan rights against colonial powers. He was even accused of sedition by the British government, when he supported a Samoan chief, but was eventually hailed as a peacemaker. He worked as hard as ever, even after settling in Valima, in 1890, his estate in Samoa.

Stevenson must be well remembered for his empathy and understanding of ethnic people, not only Chinese, but also other immigrant groups. These days, there are constant stories of streets, monuments, and schools that were named after someone prominent only to discover they had xenophobic outlooks.

It should be noted that the Chinese were not quite as understanding as Stevenson. This was especially true of their attitudes and treatment of women. Another example is, even though the Chinese Benevolent Association did much to protect the rights of sojourners, they lent money at usurious rates of four to eight percent, per month. Robert Louis Stevenson has a great lesson to teach everyone about being empathetic.

ROBERT LOUIS STEVENSON MEMORIAL
Designed by Bruce Porter and Willis Polk in 1897.

By way of memorialization, standing near the northwest corner of Portsmouth Square is a majestic monument to RLS, designed by Bruce Porter and Willis Polk in 1897. It would be easy enough to get a photo of the monument. When parking at the underground Portsmouth Square Garage, it is one of the first things one sees upon exiting the elevator. This old image has been chosen because it shows a Chinese gentleman and a small child viewing it. It is a reminder that in addition to being one of the most famous writers in history, RLS also showed empathy and understanding for the thousands of Chinese who lived surrounding Portsmouth Square. The photo also is a reminder of the time a young Chow Chong and his uncle Fook Tane befriended him. Still, little is written about RLS's Chinatown encounters.

RLS's words were descriptive not only of the plight of sojourners but also of Native Americans, African Americans, and those of the Jewish faith. It was too bad politicians didn't listen to him. Here, RLS is remembered not only as a legendary writer but also as a man who embodied empathy and understanding toward oppressed people. For Chow Chong, the voyage with Stevenson was a coming-of-age event. He had just joined his father and uncle in the funeral business at the age of fourteen. One of his first adventures was near the town of Sonora in the Gold Country. It was a harrowing experience. Lennie wrote:

> *Chinese gold miners. They hauled the funeral house … by horse and carts up the San Diego Hills from San Francisco. … Granduncle Ning Choie Tane asked my Father Chow Chong to help him rebuild the disassembled Ning Yung's funeral house and living quarters on one of the empty lots near Chinatown. But they had problems getting a permit to reassemble it.*

> *Around 1880, my Father and a couple of his friends went prospecting for gold in the San Diego Hills, near Angel Camp and China Camp. They re-assembled the funeral house there … and planned to build a Chinese temple … the miners in the area … Chinese youth watched with*

interest as they rebuilt the building with the materials they'd painfully brought along.

Upon completion of the funeral house, several hostile Whites moved in, evicted them, and threatened to shoot them if they gave any resistance—three youth fled to the safety of an Indian settlement. In the old days, Indians assumed that Chinese, with their long queues and tanned skin, was just another tribe of Indians who spoke a different dialect and had the same problems with Whites. The Indians fed, protected my father and his friends, getting them to the Chinese Camp near Jamestown. The San Diego Hills are now part of Columbia College, Columbia. Chong continued to crew for the family seafaring business.

When he was around twenty, Chow sailed with his father and his uncle Fook Tane on one of their Chinese Junks with a shipload of dried shrimps, scallops, and abalone … Chow's first trip to China with his father took only two months, but it was almost eight months to get back to the Bay Area.

On their return trip, poor weather conditions forced them to sail toward the Fiji Islands and Samoa, where they found fellow Clansmen and stayed for several months. While there, … Chow purchased several hundred pounds of dried shark fins and ginger before setting sail to California. Shark fins and ginger were Chinese delicacies that were offered at a good price.

CHAPTER 9
The Extraordinary Junk

It isn't clear exactly how often the Clan and crew took their voyages back and forth to Kwong Hoy. Lennie mentioned four trips but there were likely several more because part of their enterprise was returning remains to China presumably every few years and returning with hard-to-get items in Chinatown. Included in the returns were sojourners from Kwong Hoy who wanted to come to Gum San, but desired to avoid the exorbitant fees charged by the Six Companies. The first sailing to settle in America came in the 1840s, and subsequent returns in the 1890s showed they sailed for a half century.

The description of Chong's first trip would have involved sailing a total distance of 15,000 nautical miles. A nautical mile is equivalent to 1.1508 miles on land which means the trip was longer than 17,000 miles. This assumes they went in a straight line. However, the distance would have been greater, if they needed to use a zig zag sailing method called tacking, to go against the wind.

Combined with routine sailings back and forth to Monterey from San Francisco—about 180 nautical miles—the total distance approached about 200,000 nautical miles. In short, the Clan with their two sailing vessels were one of the greatest seafarers in history. Perhaps their best achievement was surviving those trips. An equally interesting fact is that in addition to the distance sailed, trips were taken in their wooden vessels—Junks.

An average person is familiar with those vessels sailed by Columbus and other explorers during the Age of Discovery, roughly the 15th through 17th centuries. I must point out that the U.S. curriculum is slanted toward Western Civilization and Eastern Civilization receives less coverage. Most history students would be familiar with European style sailing vessels.

A REPLICA OF COLUMBUS' SANTA MARIA
Courtesy of Wikipedia Commons.

CHINESE JUNK CIRCA 1900
Courtesy of Wikipedia Commons.

A less familiar sailboat would be the Junk. Yet, it is one of the most interesting ships in history.

Wikimedia expounded on the origin of the term Junk. It is an English word that comes from Portuguese *junco* and from Malay *jong*. The basic design of the Junk dates back to the second century AD, almost 2,000 years. Its innovations include the rudder placed at the rear, a unique sail using horizontal battens which allows for adjustment of surface area, and a flat bottom for sailing in shallow water. Most important of all were the use of sealed watertight compartments between the framework known as bulkheads.

This meant that if one section should fill with water, the ship was resistant to sinking. History shows that one of the major problems the famous ocean liner Titanic had in 1912 was the bulkheads didn't entirely seal its compartments. (Wikipedia: https://en.wikipedia.org.np.)

It is hard to believe that a wooden ship could last for decades sitting in seawater. Chinese junks built in the San Francisco Bay Area were made from native Redwood which is on the soft side and thus not likely to survive the kind of use the Clan had for their vessels. Especially significant is the type of wood used to build the Clan Junks, which are made from teakwood found in South and Southeast China.

In his book, historian John Makepeace (2017) says, teak wood has become the wood of ships. The wood is known as ironwood in China because teak grows harder with age. (*Encyclopedia of Wood*. U S Department of Agriculture.)

Chinese seafarers found that by burying teak in the damp ground for several years, they could expand the strength and resistance of the teak to almost all marine and land parasites as well as to weather conditions. This treatment was used on wood intended for hard duty use such as boats and marine building.

The inherent oiliness of the wood acts as a natural protectant. While other woods rot from the water, teak has always been used for shipbuilding. Other marine uses included bulwarks, hulls, hatches, planking, oars, and masts. "Properly treated teak is harder than iron and comparable to steel" (Understanding The Properties of Teak Wood, May 26, 2020, np).

Another interesting characteristic was the ease with the story of the Amoy. The Junk Amoy story lends credence to the notion that the design of the Junk indeed made it a seaworthy vessel. George Waard commissioned the building of a Junk in 1922. Although this would have been about eight years before the Chows and Nings sailed, the design of the boat was substantially unchanged from those built hundreds of years before. Waard had commissioned the ship to use as a floating museum to show the seaworthiness of the junk. In 1922 the Amoy sailed across the Pacific Ocean from China to Victoria, British Columbia in eighty-seven days. The crew consisted of George Waard, his Chinese wife, Choyee, and their ten-year-old son who served as navigator, and three Chinese crewmen. The crew returned to China shortly after their arrival on the West Coast. This story is noteworthy because it showed that a family could sail on board.

THE AMOY CIRCA 1922
Courtesy of Wikipedia Commons.

THE WAARD FAMILY AND CREW
Courtesy of www.roxanagraphs.us.

THE FREE CHINA SAILING IN SAN FRANCISCO BAY
Courtesy of Wikipedia Commons.

THE VOYAGE OF THE FREE CHINA

Another example about the ease with which a Junk could be operated was the story of Free China. In 1955, six adventurous young men sailed an old Junk they had acquired from Keelung, Taiwan, to San Francisco. Between them, they had virtually no sailing experience but had worked as fishermen on Trawlers. One person had come along to film the event. The voyage contained many fits and starts but they eventually arrived in San Francisco amid much fanfare.

After languishing for a while it was brought back to Keelung, Taiwan, where it now stands as a monument to sailing history.

SEAWORTHY JUNKS OF THE CLAN

There are no verified pictures of the Clan's two Junks but there are examples of the type they would have sailed. The picture below is a view of a large Junk at Rincon Cove. Below is an ocean-going junk anchored at a Chinese fishing village at Point San Bruno in 1899, further south from the Rincon Point fishing village.

RINCON POINT FISHING VILLAGE
Courtesy of OpenHistory.org.

CHAPTER 10
Wild West Stories

Besides sailing the high seas, the Wild West was another enterprise involving the Clan. In the mid-1880s, Tombstone, Arizona, which the Chinese called Sek Bei became a boomtown due to the discovery of silver ore, and involvement came from rattlesnakes.

In just a few years, the population grew rapidly from 500 to over 14,000. Estimates of the Chinese population during that period range from a high of around 500 to a low of 120. Initially, the reason for the presence of Chinese in Tombstone was participation in silver mining. There was a bustling Chinese community known as Hoptown.

Besides residents, hundreds more Chinese laborers from the surrounding area often came to Hoptown for supplies, relaxation, and gambling. A significant portion originates in the Kwong Hoy region.

Chinese herbal medicine has an unusual ointment called Heung May Sear, a kind of liniment used to relieve joint and muscle pain. This is something hard working sojourners would have needed, and many brought the potion with them on their journey to Gum San. It was made by putting a kind of serpent found in rice paddies called the Water Snake into a jar filled with liquor. For some reason, herbalists decided the snake must be put in the jar alive. It was a common medicine in China; despite widespread demand for the ointment, a problem developed. There were no rice paddies and no water snakes in America.

Some enterprising Chinese in Tombstone got what they thought was a bright idea. There were plenty of rattlesnakes in the area, and perhaps they could substitute. It took quite a while before it was realized the substitute snake did not have the same effect. It turned out that water snakes were high in Omega-3 fatty acids, which had a good medicinal effect. Rattlesnakes did not have nearly as much of the compound.

SNAKE WINE
Courtesy of Wikipedia Commons.

Lennie wrote about the Clan's Chinese association in Tombstone and their enterprises.

Tombstone's Chinese were known for their business in peddling live Heung May Sear ... or Rattlesnake Alcohol drink, which was said to give strength, energy, and vitality. The concoction was especially favored by gung fu enthusiasts and Tongmen.

After several Tombstones Sek Bei Chinese came to Choie Tane's business on Dupont Street in San Francisco to sell him Heung May Sear, rattlesnake potion, they also came to help Jub Gwuck at their cemetery. Great-Great Granduncle Choie Tane and Chow began taking periodic trips on the Wells Fargo Express and trains to southwest Chinatowns. They delivered parcels and Jub Gwuck from their holding cemeteries, bringing them back to San Francisco for reburial in China.

Choie Tane and Chow Chong brought along the necessary ancestral worshipping supplies and helped the Chinese with ancestral respect rituals at their Tombstone temple and cemetery. The two made Heung Yow or Incense and Oil donations at the temple and helped the worshippers place tiny cups of wine, bowls of rice, boiled chicken, and barbecued pork in front of the tombstones.

They burned paper replicas of material things, such as clothing, furniture, and money; they also lighted incense and ornately colored red candles, kowtowed three times before their forebears, and wished them a good and peaceful life in the after land.

Then, they checked and touched up the names and addresses in Chinese characters on the wooden tombstones to pledge the bodies would be delivered to the right destinations in China. Because many of the deceased came from small and secluded villages on the summits of the mountains, She Yup ... [and] Four Counties of Southern Canton province, they asked detailed questions to identify the specific locations of the many isolated villages.

RITUALS AT TOMBSTONE CEMETERY

Courtesy of Wikipedia Commons.

Before the bodies were exhumed, cleaned up, and shipped to China, they were buried in holding cemeteries for years. The Clan prepared sojourner bodies for return to Kwong Hoy.

Providing funerals was not an easy business. Even after death, indignities were heaped upon the remains that ranged from grave robbing to inhumane disposal. The story of Old Chap is an example of the problems they encountered.

Tombstone's historian emeritus, Ben Traywick, wrote an "Old Chap Story" to document one of many incidents in the historical record detailing racism against the Chinese (indearizona. com, 11/9/2017). "Traveling by train in Yuma with a box of bones in his hands," G.W. Chapman did what many believed to be sacrilegious. He dumped a huge box filled with dead Chinese immigrants' bones into the Colorado River (indearizona.com 11/9/2017 np).

It was a warm day in 1882, and Old Chap, Tombstone's express messenger and mail clerk, had promised their families that he would fulfill the cultural tradition of returning the bones to their homeland. His violation of the cultural tradition was one of many incidents across Arizona in which Chinese were treated as second-class citizens.

In the 19th century, Chinese emigrated to the United States in large numbers and helped modernize America by building railroads. Their customs and lifestyle unsettled Whites, who used the power of legislation and general hate to discriminate against them. On the day of disposal, Chapman could care less about tradition. Upon returning to Tombstone, he lost his job, but his misdeeds later paid off. He ran for Tombstone's city assessor, and the local paper said the bone-dumping insulted Chinese residents in the area.

He took little time to reply with an insensitive remark: "Yes, I did dump the damn Chinamen into the river; and if I had it to do over again, I would throw every damn Chinaman, alive or dead, into the Colorado River that came into Arizona." He won the largest majority of anyone in Tombstone's history (np., March 2022).

CHINA MARY

Tombstone was dominated by an interesting woman, Ah Chun, better known to locals as *China Mary*. The place in which she lived was described as follows:

> Hoptown, where all the Chinese lived, took up one square block on one end of town and was honeycombed with alleys and tunnels. It was so named because it appeared to the townspeople that Chinese hopped in and hopped out. China Mary, who was usually adorned in fine silk robes and brilliant jade jewelry, owned and operated a general store located in the heart of Hoptown. Mary's store dealt in both American and Chinese merchandise. In that role, China Mary quickly gained a reputation as a universal accommodator (https://en.wikipedia.org/wiki/China_Mary, Retrieved March 28, 2025).

Everyone knew that nothing in Hoptown was done without China Mary's go-ahead so she was held in high esteem throughout Tombstone society. She was an organized and shrewd business operator who had the attitude that discourse was bad for business. Her private police force handled problems that arose within her community and was much feared by the round-eyes, or Whites.

To illustrate her importance, Lennie wrote about the movie named *China Mary*.

> *The movie-makers version of China Mary buried at the restored Bullhead Cemetery was a non-specific generic name for Chinese women in America, which carried racial prejudice and derogatory connotations. The term China Mary was akin to John Chinaman for Chinese men, but worse being subservient-servile Chinese women during the Wild West Days.*
>
> *The unfavorable nickname or sobriquet to have led solitary, dismal, and inharmonious lives from Alaska to Wyoming. We all knew that early history of Chinese*

Americans had been recorded in haphazard and biased manners, and Chinese themselves added to the confusion by changing names, birthdates, etc., whatever the occasions called for. Tombstone City and Cochise County historical records showed a Mary Sing Choy with several birth dates ranging between 1833 to 1850.

Mary Sing Choy read and wrote English, and was active in Tombstone community affairs, owned real estate properties, and had bank accounts. It may not be a China Mary in the generic sense, but ... like my father Chow Chong, she must've learned English in a missionary school and, having associated with White teachers, felt comfortable straddling Eastern and Western cultures. She accepted the name, Mary, a given or chosen Christian name, ... a practice among English-speaking Chinese girls.

MARY SING CHOY (AKA CHINA MARY)

Note: Although the photo above is often attributed to be that of Mary Sing Choy, researcher Sandy Chan (sandychan.net) has indicated it is not likely her.

WHY TOMBSTONE?

There was apparently another reason for the large Chinese population in Tombstone—the Chinese Exclusion Laws. In 1882, Congress passed the Asian Exclusion Act, and this has been the only instance where a specific ethnic group was barred from immigration and subject to deportation on the basis of race. Despite agitation from people like Denis Kearny and numerous politicians, massive Chinese immigration took place from the 1850s through the 1870s. During those decades, tens of thousands of Chinese journeyed across the Pacific, drawn to mining jobs sparked by the California Gold Rush and construction jobs provided by the Central Pacific Railroad. The work was dangerous, and poorly paid, but Chinese immigrants, facing poverty, conflict, and famine in their homeland, found the opportunities in America worth the risk.

A family in China could be kept out of poverty if a Chinese immigrant sent them one-quarter of the most meager wage. Exploiting Chinese immigrants' willingness to work, American employers often hired them instead of White workers, whose unions demanded far higher wages.

These Exclusion Laws prohibited Chinese laborers from entering the United States and called for the deportation of sojourners already in the country. A few exceptions were mainly for those who were merchants or temporary visitors. The law was to last ten years but was extended indefinitely with the passage of the Geary Act in 1892. The restriction would last until 1943, and even then, there would be limits with the use of quotas until 1965, when immigration laws were changed.

During this time of persecution, White workers—infuriated by the labor competition and emboldened by widely held anti-Chinese racist and eugenic sentiments—retaliated against Chinese with violence and political activism. The United States has an unfortunate history of treating ethnic immigrants badly, which continues to the present. Nonetheless, Joke Sings were able to become citizens despite the hardships. Still, when law was passed, it made it difficult for sojourners who were in China. If they were laborers, it was nearly impossible for them to return. Basically, only merchants and their families were allowed to travel back and forth. A severe bind was placed on the labor-procuring operations of the Six Companies and their clients.

This resulted in an increase in the smuggling of Chinese workers into the United States via Canada and Mexico, with Mexico having by far the greatest number of undocumented immigrants from China. Tombstone was only twenty-nine miles from the Mexican border and thus a common destination. The Six Companies did not involve themselves directly in smuggling but extended the same services they provided sojourners before 1882.

THE SUEY YING TONG OF TOMBSTONE

Lennie wrote about Chinese settlers during those wild west days. With the following she narrates their experiences.

> Many of the original Chinese who settled in the Midwest Chinatowns during the Wild West Days were members of Chee Kung Tang. The Chee Kung Tang was an anti-Ching Dynasty revolutionary organization that started in the Yangtze River area six hundred years ago. When the Ching dynasty military won the war against the Ming dynasty soldiers, many Chee Kung Tang members fled from China because they ... were beheaded if caught.

> During the 1860-80s, when White American shippers solicited Indentured Servants, or Seven Years Slaves, in the British colony of Hong Kong, the Chee Kung Tang revolutionists disguised themselves as coolies and contracted themselves to the White shippers to come to America. However, some came by Chinese Junk ships from Kwong Hoy Bay seaport.

> Once they landed on American soil, most of the revolutionists disappeared into hiding among their comrades. Also, they did not fulfill their Hong Kong Indentured Servants' labor contracts. Arizona was favored as one of the revolutionary headquarters because of its location

to the California and Mexico border, where the Chinese could run across.

In time, some of the Chee Kung Tang members formed off-shoot branches, such as the Bing Kung Tong, Hop Sing Tong, Suey Ying Tong, Suey Sing Tong, Hip Sing Tong, and so on, largely for gambling, opium, and prostitution turf purposes, wherever there was a congregation of lonely Chinese men who gambled and were potential drug addicts.

Soon, the offshoot Tong branches were fighting over the highly lucrative turf territories in … the Tong Wars. The Tongs settled their turf war through a series of meetings to divide the turf territories, as recorded in the Chinese Handbook of America in 1946.

The Suey Ying Tong acquired turf rights to Arizona with two Tong headquarters. Phoenix was in the north and Tucson in the south, with Tombstone, being near the Mexican border, and under the jurisdiction of Tucson. The main headquarters of Suey Ying Tong was in San Francisco.

Lennie reflected on the lives of her cousins, as they struggled inside the context of forced labor, but still managed to become Joke Sings.

Two of my granduncle Ning's village cousins who worked at the Ning Yung Cemetery and Funeral House had been Mai Jee Jai, Sold Like Pigs, as seven-year indentured servants or slaves to White shippers in Hong Kong and had just fulfilled their contract. They had dreamt of ending their outcast heritage by starting life anew in the United States.

After working for our Ning forbearers for a few years, a childless friend with the family name of Wong from Yuma, Arizona, adopted them as sons. When friend

Wong adopted the two young men, they could change their sai sing, or small family name, Ning, to a dai sing, or the big family name of Wong ... this was a big family name in America, it had its own family associations and benevolence. They were actively involved in Arizona's Chinese community politics.

CHAPTER 11
Little Pete Must Die

THE ASSASSINATION

In his 1962 book, *The Hatchet Men,* noted historian Richard Dillon described Fong Ching, also known as Little Pete, as a totally amoral Chinatown crime kingpin. His gangland style murder in a barbershop chair is part of one of the most infamous crime stories in Chinatown history. The crime was never solved, although two suspects, Lem Jung and Chew Tin Gop, were said to have escaped to China. Lennie heard from Chow Chong—her father—that Suey Ying Tong was actually involved.

Lennie wrote about the corruption and abuse of that case.

> *Fong Ching, an urbanite suede-shoe-boy from Hong Kong who learned to speak English at a Chinatown missionary school, became involved with bribing horse-racing jockeys to win bets on races; he was caught and sent to jail.*

FONG CHING, A SKETCH OF LITTLE PETE
Courtesy of San Francisco Call/California Digital Newspaper Collection.

Rogue police and corrupt politicians took advantage of his arrest and psychologically prepared him to be placed in Chinatown after his release, as their dupe, stool pigeon, and inter-state-controlled gang leader.

The rogue police and pork-barrel politicians wanted to take full control of and extort the Chinatown's underworld syndicate. The police had provided Hooligan Fong Ching with a White bodyguard as protection and as a warning to the Chinatown folks to leave Fong Ching alone or suffer the consequences of White rage. Confident that no one in Chinatown would dare harm him, Fong Ching became arrogant as he walked around Chinatown with his White guard.

During the 1895 San Francisco Fair at Golden Gate Park, Hooligan Fong Ching, a city slicker, police dupe, and stool pigeon, became involved with the international kidnapping of Chinese girls from Hong Kong and China to dance at the Park's events. He also contracted with Chicago Chinatown's criminal elements and corrupt police, and after the Golden Gate Park Fair, he … personally delivered Chinese dancers to them, to become prostitutes.

One of the kidnapped girls was a Hoy Sun Clan cousin of Arizona's Suey Ying Tong headman who lived in Tucson; Tucson's Chinese population was substantially 100 percent Hoy Sun folks. Upon learning that his young cousin was one of the girls kidnapped and had been forced to perform at Golden Gate Park and then sent to Chicago's underworld to become a prostitute, Suey Ying Tong offered an enticing reward … to kill Fong Ching.

The Arizona Suey Ying Tong men wanted to use the assassination of Hooligan Fong Ching … to give an unspoken warning to the rapscallion law enforcement, as to what would happen if they ever utilized Chinatown's mobsters to kidnap Chinese women for prostitution and other illegal purposes. A couple of Tombstone's Hoy Sun Tong members accepted the offer to kill Fong Ching and chose Chinese New Year, January 23, 1897.

Before the assassination, San Francisco's Yellow Journalism news media were forewarned about the impending murder. Thus, the newspaper reporters were at the murder scene minutes after the killing. Yellow Journalists front-paged and sensationalized the unsolved assassination throughout the country for months and newspapers sold many copies.

Since 1897, these journalists and their ensuing publishers have re-issued and re-sensationalized the "unsolved assassination" dozens of times because many newspapers and magazines were sold. For example, the Examiner Newspaper, dated January 23, 1897, printed the sensational news entitled, "The murder of Fong Ching, alias Little Pete." On February 6, 1995, it was again re-issued by deputy police Chief Kevin Mullen, almost a hundred years later during the Chinese New Year.

When Fong Ching was murdered in 1897, the Chinatown folks kept up their Chinese New Year celebrations, which included a spirited colorful parade, for two more weeks. When questioned by the police, Chinatown folks claimed no knowledge of the murder.

Suey Ying Tong elders told the story that the Tombstone killers chose January 23, 1897, during the Chinese New Year celebration, when there were a lot of out-of-towners and strangers in the City as the right time to assassinate Fong Ching and leave town unnoticed.

Before the Tombstone's killers set off to San Francisco, other Tombstone Tong members had already made reservations at their local Chinatown restaurant and purchased several cases of firecrackers to celebrate. Upon hearing from their fellow tong men via their newly installed community telephone that Fong Ching had been killed, the Tombstone Chinese celebrated by setting off their large cache of firecrackers, which took them several hours to burn; they then feasted for two weeks. Great-grandfather Albert Bew Chan, Lucretia's grandfather, said that he was the ten-year-old messenger boy who delivered the killers' message via their Chinatown telephone switchboard to Tombstone that Fong Ching had been killed.

CHAPTER 12
Filial Piety

1895: THE MIGRATION BACK TO KWONG HOY

Chow Chong very much wanted to be a Joke Sing. By 1895, it became evident that his father's failing health would force his return to the home village. The concept of Filial Piety called for the welfare of his parents to be the number one priority, especially since he was an only child. It was the last instance of the Clans' voyages back and forth to China on their own Junk.

Lennie wrote a story about the China return.

Chow returned to Kwong Hoy to live with and take care of his elderly parents during the early 1900s; he married the girl his parents had selected, but life was not very peaceful. There were serious problems with bandits, and being from America, he and his parents were considered wealthy Overseas Chinese, and had to contend with people constantly asking for hand-outs.

The whole district of Hoy Sun had to deal with bandits from the highlands as well as pirates from the ocean. His wife was killed during one of the pirate invasions, and a year later he married my mother, Ning Shee.

While living in Kwong Hoy, Great-grandfather Chow built a stone wall around their property and also helped build a couple of turrets and cannons for community protection. Night watchers were hired to Da Gong or hit the Gongs at designated hours to tell the sleeping community that all was well.

Chong's first wife, chosen by his parents, was indicative of the family status. She had bound feet and was killed in a pirate raid. There was a one-eyed woman pirate named Ying Don who attacked the Kwong Hoy villagers both by land and by sea.

Chong's heart was clearly in America. Shortly after getting his parents settled, he returned to San Francisco. It was the first trip any member of the Clan had taken by conventional steamship rather than by the family Junk. Chong worked for a while, then traveled back to Kwong Hoy in 1904. It was fortunate timing because he missed the 1906 earthquake and fire. However, Chong returned in 1907.

That was when he lived a horrible experience during a stay at the Detention Shed.

DETENTION SHED IN ANGEL ISLAND
Courtesy of The Bancroft Library, University of California, Berkeley.

Before 1892, arrivals to San Francisco were detained on the ships that carried them and were interviewed on board to determine whether a person had the right to enter the country.

With the advent of the 1882 Chinese Exclusion Act, these interviews became unwieldy, and a Shed on the Pacific Mail Steamship Company docks was converted into holding facilities. The Shed experience was dehumanizing. As many as 500 immigrants were crowded in the shed while awaiting interviews.

THE SHED'S INTERIOR
Courtesy of Wikipedia Commons.

An article in the San Francisco Call dated 1908 covered the situation:

> For years, the Chinese have protested against the conditions at the Mail dock, where they declared they were herded like sheep and treated like prisoners. ... The detention shed has been the scene of historic occurrences in the annals of San Francisco.

> During the Denis Kearny agitation a mob attacked the place one night and burned part of the shed. A riot followed, in which the Chinese and members of the mob engaged in a general battle. Upon several occasions, they attempted to break from the place, and they became so frequent that a big fire hose was brought into play and used to subdue them (San Francisco Call, Volume 104, Number 64, 3 August 1908, np).

With the recognition that the Shed was not a good option, the Immigration Service built a new facility in the largest one, Angel Island in San Francisco Bay, and thus it became the ideal site because the facility was accessible only by boat. It would be safe from rioters, with the capacity to detain incoming immigrants until their status was determined, which became a big issue. The Angel Island Immigration Station opened in 1910.

ANGEL ISLAND IMMIGRATION STATION
Courtesy of The Bancroft Library, University of California, Berkeley.

Angel Island is found on the northside of San Francisco Bay, near the town of Tiburon. Before acceptance or rejection into the Country, arrivals from Asia were offloaded at the Station for processing. It would be comparable to Ellis Island where European immigrants were processed. However, because of the 1882 Chinese Exclusion Act, and subsequent extensions, the Station became a checkpoint for barring Chinese immigrants, unless they met qualifications for exceptions to the Acts.

The 1906 earthquake had a profound effect on those wishing to enter the country. The Earthquake and subsequent fires resulted in the destruction of all city records. Residents of the city were instructed to come in and register. During this time some Chinese residents saw an opportunity. When they registered, they indicated they had family in China, even though that wasn't necessarily the case. They listed one or more sons, sometimes daughters. The objective was to create slots which would allow others to immigrate under the rules of the Chinese Exclusion Act. Paper identities were sold to those who wished to work in America. Clearly a larcenous activity, this was the way laborers escaped the horrors. Besides natural, political, and economic disasters, during the Taiping Rebellion from 1850 to 1864 alone, an estimated 20 million people were killed. Thus, their desire to come to Gum San was immense, and the business of selling identities became profitable business.

SAN FRANCISCO CITY HALL, AFTER THE 1906 EARTHQUAKE
Courtesy of Wikipedia Commons.

As immigration authorities learned of the practice, they conducted interviews to assess if an arrival was a paper son. The practice of keeping records of the interviews was begun so that the information could be cross-referenced to later arrivals who said they were from the same village. If the answers did not match, the applicants were rejected and deported.

A side benefit for descendants was that all the records were saved and made available for everyone to see at the National Archives in San Bruno, California. For offspring of those early intrepid arrivals, these archives are a treasure trove of information.

When daughters Meredith and Alison visited, they came away with more than 300 pages of interviews forebears gave. Documents available from those days are truly invaluable.

TYPICAL "INTERVIEW"
Courtesy of the National Archives Collection, San Bruno.

1920—RETURN TO GUM SAN

A major family migration occurred in 1920 when Chong decided he would return to America. His parents had both passed, and he no longer had a reason to stay. This was a major endeavor because he had his second wife, Ning See, two sons, and a daughter to bring.

One indication Chow Chong intended to return to America was that he assigned Americanized names to his children. Thus, Chow Hem Look became Henry Look Chew, and Woy Guey was named Jerry Chew. Chow Guoi Lee was named Rose.

Because Jerry was born in China, there was a ten-year space between him and his siblings. Their stay at Angel Island was traumatic, lasting over a year. The family was under major suspicion.

The Exclusion Act was in full force, convincing immigration authorities that allowing entrance to a whole family was a problem. However, Chong was a laborer and there were only exclusions for merchants. His right to entry was based on the fact that he was a natural-born citizen. That right was based on a well-known case in 1898, Wong Ark Kim v the United States.

The problem was that in 1892, with the passage of the Geary Act, Chinese persons were required to carry a Certificate of Residency on them at all times or be subject to deportation. The Six Companies protested this and told people not to comply with the requirement. They also called for donations to fight the case in court. Chong went along and did not bother to get a certificate. Thousands did not file for it.

However, the Six Companies lost the case, and people like Chong were stuck without a certificate. It didn't actually seem like a big problem initially. Chong traveled to China without an ID. Because he was very Americanized, Chong was given entry, when a White witness testified that he was a natural-born citizen. However, gaining entry with five other people proved difficult. Thus, the family stayed at the Immigration Station for over a year.

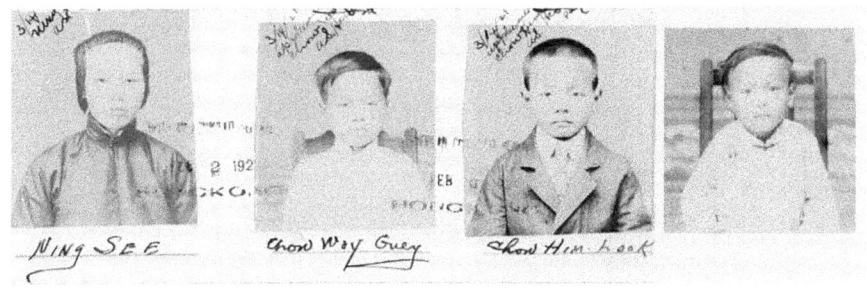

ROSE, JERY, HENRY, AND LENNIE
Family archives.

Lennie captured the difficulties experience by those who lived through these interrogations.

At Angel Island, the Chow family was interrogated by immigration officials; the children were separated from the adults ... His two sons, Granduncle Jerry and Granduncle Henry Look, matched their parents' answers, but their daughter, Grandaunt Rose Ha Peng, the youngest of the three children, missed a couple of questions, which caused the interrogators to detain the family at Angel Island for several months; the interrogators concluded that Grandaunt Rose Ha Peng was not their child, but the daughter of someone else they were trying to bring into the Country. One of the questions was, "Was there a lake behind your house in China?" The two boys and parents answered

95

"No," but their daughter—Grandaunt Don Quei Ha Peng said, "Yes."

In the old days, the Chows, as fishermen, dug a large pond behind their house to breed and to keep fish alive before selling them. To a small child, the large fishpond was a lake.

Thus, concluding that Rose was not their child, she was deported. The officials also questioned great-grandfather Chow's citizenship as an American-born citizen.

Great-Grandfather Chow sought help from his former employer, the Halstead Funeral House, and from two former teachers at the Presbyterian Missionary School. He also produced records that he had voted a number of times as an American-born citizen. His English fluency helped.

In 1928, as a teenager, the family endeavored to bring Rose over. Again Chow Chong worked hard to gain her release, after several months of detention. In the eyes of the interrogators, she was a young female. That was problematic.

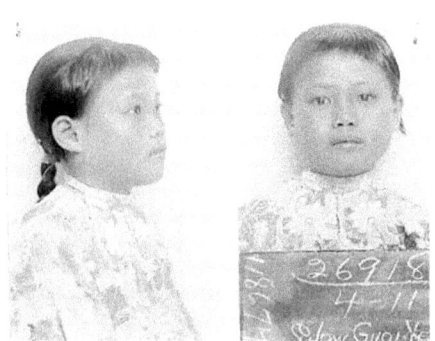

ROSE, 1928
Family archives.

Rose actually was more fortunate than most deportees. She married a hard-working peasant farmer named Peng and became Rose Ha Peng.

With the rise of Communist China after the War, the farm they worked on became part of a commune. The Cultural Revolution resulted in the deaths of millions, but Rose and her husband Peng were lucky to be low-level peasants who worked very hard. Peng was eventually put in charge of the commune, which allowed his son Peng Kuo Wah to become educated. Kuo Wah eventually became a Deputy Economic Minister in Southeast China, an important position in the emerging People's Republic of China. Peng Kuo Wah became one of the directors of the building of the city of Shenzhen, adjacent to Hong Kong. And the whole family lived a comfortable life by Chinese standards. It also gave Lennie and her husband, Harry, opportunities to visit.

Lennie made a total of eight trips to China; the first was in the 1970s, even before President Richard Nixon's historic visit in 1972. It was also helpful that Clan descendant Roberta Chew—her father is Jerry—her niece, and my cousin was a United States Deputy Counsel stationed in Beijing. It is ironic that a descendant of the Clan ascended to this high position in China. Rose's granddaughters visited the United States in the 1990s. She eventually relocated to Vancouver, Canada.

LOOK CHEW: THE LAST SEAFARER

Chow Him Look, otherwise known as Henry, was born in 1910 from Chow Chong's first wife. He had an older brother who separately emigrated to America; little is known about him. Henry was close to Chong and his second family. He worked hard to support the whole group, especially after the family bought the house located at 1060 Washington. Henry worked at a fish processing facility in Alviso and often worked as a crew member on fishing boats that sailed to Alaska. His love of the sea eventually led him to work on steamships sailing the Pacific.

With the outbreak of World War II, he joined the merchant marines. A dangerous duty. Between 1939 and 1945, 9,521 merchant mariners lost their lives. According to the National World War II Museum, this was a higher proportion than those killed in any military branch. Sadly, in September 1943, Henry was killed in an air raid off of the coast of New Guinea.

One of Lennie's older brothers, Frank, was an infantryman for one of the Island-Hopping units. When he got word of Henry's death, Frank went to Guadalcanal, where casualties were held, to identify the body and planned for burial at the National Cemetery in Honolulu. Sadly, his father passed away a few months earlier, in 1943, and Chow Chong never knew his son's fate. It was the end of an era. Henry Look Chew was the last seafarer of the Clan.

HENRY LOOK CHEW, 1919
Family archives.

PART III

LENNIE'S STORY

IN HER JOURNAL, LIN KIM LENNIE LEE,
NÉE CHOW, PROVIDED THE HISTORY
OF HER NAME: *"MINERS GAVE THEIR
CHILDREN NAMES RELATING TO GOLD,
SUCH AS MY FATHER GIVING ME THE NAME
LIN KIM, MEANING WITH GOLD. AT THE
TIME OF MY BIRTH, FATHER, DURING ONE
OF HIS FISHING TRIPS FROM MONTEREY
TO ALASKA, PURCHASED ALASKAN GOLD
STOCKS AND WAS HOPING THEY
WERE A FRUITFUL INVESTMENT."*

CHAPTER 13
BADASSES

Jade Snow Wong's *Fifth Chinese Daughter* is one of the best-known autobiographies written by an American woman of Chinese descent. It chronicled her life from birth in 1922 to 1945, describing what it was like to grow up in a traditional household in San Francisco's Chinatown. She excelled in college, graduated first in her class at Mills, became a Phi Beta Kappa, and a famous ceramicist. Her book was so well received by the general public, that in 1954, the State Department organized a tour designed to show how well Chinese American women were doing. The goal was to improve relations with Asian countries after World War II.

No Chinese Stranger was published in 1975 and focused on her later life and times. Most recently, she has been criticized by critics and academics, assigning her the ideal type of Model Minority which actually implicates stereotypic aspects. In context of the times, Jade Snow Wong excelled.

L K LENNIE LEE (FIRST DAUGHTER) VERSUS
JADE SNOW WONG (FIFTH DAUGHTER)

L K Lennie Lee photograph courtesy of family archives. Jade Snow Wong portrait courtesy of Wikipedia.org.

Her father and mother, Hong and Hing Kwai Tong Wong, were classic sojourners. Father was the unquestioned patriarch. He operated a sewing factory in Chinatown and clung to tradition. He was a stern father for whom "Eating Bitterness" was a way of life. Because he was in the clothing manufacturing business, he and his family were exempt from the 1882 Chinese Exclusion Act. In typical sojourner fashion, his first priority was to see to the success of his sons. It wasn't that he didn't want his daughters to become Joke Sing, his priority was to allot his limited resources to his sons.

Jade wasn't barred from succeeding; she just had to do it alone, and earned her money working as a domestic, but was allowed to keep her earnings to finance her education. At a time when the concept didn't have negative connotations, she was a model minority. In her second book, *No Stranger,* she did not refer to herself as a "bamboo node," rather Joke Sing, she thought that was rude.

Modern-day writers and critics tend to denigrate her work, but in the context of the times it is revolutionary. In fact, modern-day portrayals of Asians depict Chinese in two ways. First, as martial arts masters. Such portrayals are good enough to win Academy Awards, so maybe an ordinary story about a young woman rising above isn't so interesting. Second, root culture portrayals that emphasize Chinese heritage people as perpetual foreigners.

Jade Snow Wong is an example of success. Despite her upbringing and the circumstances that were opposite to that of Ms. Wong's, Lennie was equally successful in her own right. Although, she did not achieve the same notoriety.

L K LENNIE LEE—FIRST DAUGHTER

Lennie was born in 1923 to Chow Chong and Ning Shee. She was the first Chinese daughter, and the middle child of nine. It's not clear that Lennie and Jade knew each other. However, Jade's father-in-law Ong Foon and Chong were friends who lived in buildings next to each other on a small street facing Portsmouth Square. The two men often traveled to Alaska together to work on fishing fleets.

As a young girl, those who knew Lennie wouldn't have given her much chance for success or survival. She was precocious and headstrong, traits not always appreciated by a struggling Chinese family during the Depression. The family first lived in the back of a building that was the headquarters for the Suey Ying Tong, on Grant Avenue, in San Francisco.

Her father, Chow Chong, rented space in a multi-story building because it was reasonable. Its membership offered a measure of protection. He was not a highbinder or gangster, but his excellent seventy-three wars were largely over, albeit some nefarious activities, such as opium distribution and prostitution were part of his survival.

Lennie wrote about the restrictive environment in which she was raised. She recalled her early upbringing.

> *During the mid-1920s, most hospitals, including San Francisco General, were largely restricted to non-Whites. Thus, most Chinese babies of my era were home-born. In fact, all of my American-born siblings, including me, were home-born. The building had gas lights and no electricity when we lived there. Electricity was installed during the Great Depression days of the 1930s.*
>
> *The old timers named Portsmouth Square Far Yuen, which meant Garden. They regularly met in Far Yuen … and planned much of their community activities. Far Yuen, though a half block in size with a few trees and restrictive laws, was the only open space within the once racially segregated Chinatown. It was a twelve-block area bordered by Kearney, California, Stockton, and Broadway Streets.*
>
> *The next-door corner building shown in the picture is called Sing Chong Lou. It was also a building that led from Grant Avenue to Walter U Plum Place. The Sing Chong grocery store … Shing Chong was at the corner of Clay and Grant Avenue. There was no address on the door facing Walter L. Lum Place. The Ong family … lived there … it was the entryway to the unit above. Forty years ago, it was condemned.*

The old tenement building where I was born leads from Grant Avenue to Walter U Lum Place at Portsmouth Square. The address is 812 on Grant Avenue and 11 1/2 Walter U. Lum Place on the backside. The picture I submitted was taken from the Portsmouth Square side of the building, which is a rear view of 812 Grant Avenue—it was a dark, dingy tenement building with one filthy community bathroom and one cockroach-ridden kitchen on our floor.

My parents did not make use of the kitchen nor the bathroom. For bathing, they've used a galvanized washtub, and a ... bucket was used as a toilet. They cooked on a three-burner hot plate in one corner of the room and climbed onto the roof to hang clothing.

Suey Ying Tong was located on the top floor. Suey Sing members were also known as Hatchet Men or Bor How Doi because they fought other gangs with hatchets or cleavers, so I've heard. Police Sergeant Manion came around daily to check that the Bor How Doi did not bother families.

For safety reasons, parents and the police restricted children from going in and out of the building and could only exit through the rear of the building. To enter, members of Suey Ying used the 812 Grant Avenue door.

My mother's uncle Ning was a night watchman for Wells Fargo Drayage Company on the street floor, on the Walter U. Lum Place side. Granduncle Ning lived in an area under the stairs ... which had been converted into small living quarters. Crates of materials imported from China and other parts of the Orient were usually piled high in the front part of the store—the imported items were forwarded to all parts of the United States.

On the weekends, Granduncle Ning preached at the corner of Washington Street and Grant Avenue, with the

Boom Boom Hui Band playing behind him. The Salvation Army was called the Boom Boom Hui because the band beats their drums continuously to attract attention.

We lived in Room 22. With no closets, the room was approximately 20' x 20'. My parents had placed four pieces of 9-inch by 6-foot wooden planks on a wooden horse to serve as a bed. Father built a loft over the bed for us children to sleep on.

The space under the makeshift bed was used for all sorts of storage. There was a brown leather Loveseat at one side of the room, which opened into a bed.

The room is approximately six-feet-by-six-feet and lit well. Father built a small wood-framed cabinet, aligned with wire mesh, and placed it at the light well, where milk and leftover food were placed. There is no address at the corner building next door ... Sing Chong Lou (sic) ... Sing Chong Building ... Sing Chong grocery store at the corner of Clay and Grant ... a sign reading emergency exit only ... enter at 760 or 778 Clay Street sign ... Ong Foon and his family used to live there. The door facing Walter L. Lum's was the entryway to their unit above.

Thirty years ago, the unit was condemned ... Ong Foon was a close friend of my father, Chow Chong. They hung out and found work together on Alaska fishing boats. Ong Foon was the father-in-law of Jade Snow Wong, the writer. She married one of Ong Foon's sons, Woodrow Ong. The Shing Chong building is on the left, and the Suey Ying Tong building is on the right. Note the separate entrance.

Suey Ying Tong Building

The Back of 800 Grant Ave.

BANCROFT LIBRARY THE BACKSIDE
OF THE SUEY YING TONG BUILDING
Courtesy of University of California, Berkeley.

CHAPTER 14
Suey Ying Tong Memories

Lennie's excellent recall and attention to detail was apparent in her writing. She wrote about her childhood memories and about the dangers that surrounded her and other children.

In 1927, when I was about four years of age, and the family was still living at the Suey Ying Tong Headquarters Building, I ventured into forbidden territory two floors above where we lived. I walked into a room where several men, smoking opium, were lying on a wooden bed made up of four sawhorses laid over with a dozen wooden planks.

There was no mattress on the bed. They were lying on grass mats laid over the wooden planks. Several rectangularly shaped white porcelain blocks served as their pillows. The small room had no closet and only one window faced the lightwell.

Two beautiful young Chinese girls dressed in embroidered brocade were sitting among the four men, laughing and lighting their opium pipes. The men appeared sleepy and were dressed in drab, grey, rumpled clothing. Their leathery brown skin over their sunken jaws made a strong contrast to the heavily made-up round, cheek girls. The bony hands with which the men held up opium pipes to smoke seemed to be devoid of all flesh.

The group didn't seem to find it unnatural, nor were they concerned that a small child had happened upon them. At first, they kidded if I wanted to try a puff, but they ignored me when I said, "No!" … After watching them for a few minutes, the opium odor bothered me, and I left to go downstairs.

An older, grey-haired woman sans make-up was sitting near the door. She was dressed in plain, dark gray, high-collared cotton Chinese-style clothing with frog buttons up the front of the shirt and matching gray rumpled pants. Her bare feet were placed on the bottom rung of the stool. Her well-worn black Chinese slippers laid nearby. The woman was scraping out dried opium from the bowl of the pipe with a small metal spoon. She placed the opium scraps onto a piece of white paper on a nightstand in front of her. After she was finished, she carefully folded the paper over the opium. She put it into a small, square, yellow, red and green-flowered tin can, along with the dried opium she had collected.

She was scraping quietly away oblivious to what was going around her. I think that she was purposely keeping her eyes away from the opium smokers and the girls to give them a sort of privacy.

I asked her what she would do with the opium. She told me "it was for others who could not afford the price of regular opium."

She took out something from her pocket, wrapped it in cloth and showed me a dried lemon cut in half … where she had also saved opium scrapings. I was told it was to be used as a drug for its opiate effects upon the pains and discomfort of rheumatism. I assumed that the dried lemon … would be cut into small pieces and sucked slowly in the mouth like cough drops or chewed like gumdrops to obtain its narcotic effect. The top floor housed the Suey Ying Tong headquarters. The floor below consisted of single men's rooms; somewhere in the area was the opium den.

Suey Ying Tong, in the olden days, was a fighting tong with Bo How Doy or Hatchet Men. I recalled that membership had declined over the last couple of decades, and the Tong parlor was quiet.

The Suey Ying Tong parlor had a light, olive-colored floor with a red and blue-squared design, I recalled; carved teakwood and rosewood straight-back chairs with red-embroidered cushions and several small, rectangular, less ornately carved end-tables were lined along two sides of the room.

The side facing Portsmouth Square had windows and double doors that opened into a fire escape; at the far side was a long teakwood table with a large incense urn in the center and several smaller urns at the two ends. On the table, a cylindrical tube, approximately three inches in diameter and eight inches tall, held a number of bamboo sticks with writing on them; fortunes and predictions were made by shaking out one of the bamboo sticks. The table was in front of a number of colorful gods which the tong men worshipped.

I still have a faint cigarette burn scar on the middle of my forehead, from when the Tongman at Suey Ying Tong put a cigarette out on my forehead. My mother said that I was two years old when the incident happened. She told me the cigarette ashes were still burning, clinging onto my forehead, when she saw me running in the house.

I do not recall the actual incident; it happened so fast, but I do remember standing in front of the opened door of Room 22, looking down the long, dingy, narrow, dusty-gray hallway, dimly lit only from the window facing Portsmouth Square. A small, thin man, shoulders swaying and puffing nervously on a cigarette, duck-walked from the dark shadows toward me, and suddenly, I was running back into Room 22, screaming in pain.

She wasn't alone, Lennie recalled, *that Great-grandfather Chow went upstairs to complain to the Tong leaders, telling him … that he had been unemployed for several months. He finally found seasonal work at a Monterey cannery and wanted the Tongmen to leave his family alone.*

The Tong leaders proposed that he be more generous in donating Heung Yow, or Incense and Oil, and Support and Benevolence money to the Tong periodically.

After the incident, while we were still living at the Suey Ying Tong Headquarters Building, Great-grandfather Chow donated Heung Yow to the organization; it was bribery or extortion money so that the Bo How Doy, or Hatchet men, leave his family alone.

CHAPTER 15
The Babysitter

Lennie and her brother George were cared for by an elder uncle who babysat them. She elaborated.

> *Great granduncle Ning Choie Tane was a longtime Far Yuen Ghown or Portsmouth Square hanger-on who when he was also our babysitter told stories about his youth. Being comparatively tall and a well-built Chinese, he looked quite snappish in his three-piece dark-grey tweed suit, which he had purchased for fifty cents from one of the many used clothing stores on McAllister Street. He had a mass of wiry salt-and-pepper hair, which made him look younger than his age of eighty when he babysat us during the 1920s.*

> *By White folks' standards, he was a poor man in a warm second-hand suit living under the rear stairs of a drainage agency across from Portsmouth Square, but not by Chinatown's standards. Though it was only a store-front residence, he had a place of his own—Lee Hot Plate to cook his soon for, or bowl of rice and hot yum, or salted fish, and boiled water for tea—he was respected as a businessman who spoke English.*

THE MIGRATION FROM CHINATOWN

Chong, despite his affiliation with the Tong, knew this was no place for his young family and moved out. The final straw was when an old man put out that cigarette on Lennie's forehead as she was standing in a hallway. It was too much.

Lennie wrote:

In the winter of 1928, Jack Dempsey, a White real es-
tate agent, helped ... Chong to move his family out of the
tenement building and into an old, two-story wooden
house built against the foot of a hill at the dead-end side
of Wetmore. Two weeks later, we woke up with our beds
sopping wet from the rain, which had fallen during the
night. We moved to an old yellow brick building in the
middle of Stone Street, a one-street alley. A few weeks
later, when the heavy rain continued, water soaked
through the brick walls and kitchen windows.

From the middle of Stone Street, we moved to the first
floor of 960 Washington, a concrete building at the cor-
ner of Stone Street. The 960 Washington Street residence
was once a brothel that had been closed by the police.
The building consisted of two stories of ten rooms and a
semi-basement with its own entryway at Stone Street
... Chong sublet two of the five rooms to help pay the
rent. Great-grandfather Chow spoke to real estate agent
Dempsey again, and he found us 242 Joice Street, a sev-
en-room flat. The flat ... in an alley on the top floor of a
two-story, red brick building.

JOICE STREET

Although not particularly well known, Joice Street, which was a
one-block-long alley between Sacramento and Clay Street, has an
interesting history.

Lennie provides a detailed description of the residence.

A deep red brick tenement hotel was once managed by
Japanese Americans at the corner of Joice and Clay; his
patrons were largely African Americans; on the ground
floor behind the hotel lobby forty students attended a
private Japanese school and there was a couple of sewing
factories on the Clay Street side.

In 1930, the YWCA had not yet been built; the vacant land was our play lot. When the Clay-Joice YWCA was completed around 1933, a Chinese American teacher named Miss Ng came to our house to ask Great-grandmother to help her get a job as a nursery schoolteacher ... located in the 81 basements of the YWCA. Miss Ng said she needed to recruit at least fifteen preschool children ... to get a job; Grandaunt Rosemary and Granduncle Herbert, at ages three and four, became two of the first preschool students at the YWCA nursery school. During the 1989 earthquake, the YWCA building suffered substantial damages and was sold to the Chinese Historical Society.

The Donaldina Cameron House, a shelter for Chinese girls who were forced into 'white slavery' or prostitution during the old days, was half a block away at the corner of Joice and Sacramento Street. After more than four decades of all-out cooperative endeavors by honest police, churches, local schools, family associations, and women vigilantes to unshackle the underworld's vice-hold of 'White Slavers,' 'White slavery' in Chinatown, at last it was largely eliminated during the 1930s.

Chinatown female shelter houses, such as Gum Moon on Washington Street and Cameron House, were already quiet places with just a few Chinese ladies, girls, and several elderly White women living there. One of the elderly White women gave me piano lessons; I asked her why she was living at Cameron House. She told me that she gave her life savings of $7,000 to live there for the rest of her life with room, board, and maid services.

Another time, I asked one of the Chinese women who had a nine-month-old baby how she came to America and ended up at Cameron House. She said when she was a young teenager in Hong Kong, a man riding a taxi offered her a job. And when she got into the taxi, he took her to a lady who sold her to a house of prostitution, and she was sent to America with several girls.

Great-grandfather Chow Chong asked Donaldina Cameron and Police Sergeant Jack Manion of the Chinatown Task Force to watch over his family, when he went out of town to work. He was concerned that his children would be lured into drugs and prostitution while he was away.

We lived at 242 Joice Street until 1934 when the building was sold. We were evicted without a word by the new Chinese owners—their method was to turn off the water, claiming we had a washing machine and were using too much water.

A RESCUE OF A YOUNG GIRL FROM A BUILDING
IN NOTORIOUS SAINT LOUIS ALLEY
Courtesy of Cameronhouse.org.

The picture of Donaldina Cameron, along with her interpreter on the previous page, depicts a rescue of a young girl from a building in notorious Saint Louis Alley, where young women who had been duped into becoming enslaved people or prostitutes were auctioned off to buyers who had bad intentions. Police Sergeant Jack Mannion was helpful in these efforts.

CHAPTER 16
1934: A Home at Last

Lennie captured the time Jack Dempsey counselled the Chows regarding the purchase of a home during the Depression. Lennie recalled:

Jack Dempsey suggested that Chow look for a home of his own since there were a lot of properties for sale in Chinatown. ... As an American-born, he was eligible to buy property. By then, oldest son Jerry was working for the Simon Bag Company—they made potato sacks. His employer's widow, Mrs. Annie E. Symon, was willing to sell 1016 Washington Street to Chow for $3,200. Chow made a down payment of $1,700, and Mrs. Symon carried back a first loan of $1,500 for one year.

Located in 1016 Washington, the house was a two-story rooming house occupied by Japanese who worked at one of the three Hong Sang Laundry branches at Washington and Stockton. With the help of his children, Great-grandfather Chow converted the rooming house into four units: one unit for his family, one for Granduncle Jerry, and two to rent out.

The Japanese tenants had papered the walls with layer-upon-layer of old Japanese and Chinese newspapers; it was their thrifty method of keeping the wind out of the wood-framed building. Great-grandfather Chow assigned his children jobs to help scrape the newspaper off, so he could wallpaper the walls properly. Granduncle Jerry did most of the electrical and plumbing work.

Great-grandfather paid a Jewish plumber, Mr. Cohen, and an electrician $20 each, to sign the Department of Public Works permits, thus … legalizing the property at City Hall. Those days, Chinese were not allowed to go into the plumbing and electrical business. The two plumbing companies were owned by Jewish people, Rosenbaum in Washington and Waverly, and Cohen in Stockton and Sacramento. After converting the rooming house, Great-grandfather Chow was unable to find work in San Francisco, and Granduncle Henry Look found Great-Grandfather Chow work in the cannery where he worked in Monterey, California.

GREAT-GRANDFATHER CHOW
Family archives.

Because of the Depression, when Great-Grandfather Chow, who was referred to as Chong, was nearing seventy, even though he gave his age as ten years younger, he unable to find work. Yet, no one questioned how he came up with $1,700—he would've had to work 5,000 hours. At that time, White wages were .45 and .35 cents for Blacks, respectively. With no records on Chinese, it is safe to assume he made less than .35 cents an hour.

THE GAP

Sometime around 1927, Chong went away without informing anyone of his whereabouts; his absence or the Gap was a major struggle for Ning Shee. After three years, Chong suddenly appeared. An unusual thing happened. He was able to purchase a house on Washington Street just outside Chinatown's boundary, which at the time was Powell Street. It was concluded he had found work somewhere out of town.

Later we would find out that Chong had spent three years incarcerated at the McNeil Island Federal Penitentiary in Washington State. It was a secret he kept from everyone in his family, but it was for opium dealing.

Lennie knew about this but never mentioned it to anyone. Apparently, Chong had agreed to take the rap for a Tong leader, presumably Suey Ying Tong, and did his time in jail. He was given money and thus he was able to buy a house.

ROSEMARY, HERBERT, PEGGY, FRANK, LENNIE & GEORGE
Family archives.

CHAPTER 17
Escape from Slavery

As recorded in the City and County of San Francisco, Volume 2796 Official Records, pages 95-6, and also Volume 2734, page 60, Annie E. Symon cancelled her lien. It conveyed 1016 Washington over to our Great-Grandfather on December 5, 1934.

After acquiring a home of their own, it might've been assumed that life would be better for the family. Unfortunately, that wasn't the case. Instead, it exposed Lennie to a life of servitude, perhaps even slavery.

Lennie wrote about their trials and tribulations as owners of a property. She documented,

> *Assured that the loan payoff and conveyance assignment were logged at the City Recorder's Office, Great-grandfather Chow returned to work in Monterey. A few months later, Chow received a desperate phone call from a friend, Ong Foon, that his family was being evicted from 1016 Washington Street because of the foreclosure of an unpaid loan on the property. Great-grandfather Chow did not know that Great-grandmother Ning had inadvertently put a $350 lien on the property.*

> *Great-grandmother Ning Shee was illiterate. A loan shark, E.J. (using an alias), offered her a loan of $350, subject to her signing some loan papers, witnessed by two White persons, Richard B. Bell and S. E. Herrick, as recorded ... in Book 2862, page 377; the recorded deed of trust included Great-grandfather Chow Chong's name, unsigned; Great-grandfather was out of town working in Monterey.*

> *February 26, 1935, Deed of Trust, naming E.J. as beneficiary, had a typewritten addendum, explaining*

119

said Deed of Trust as a second lien and is subordinate to the first lien in favor of Annie E. Symon, a widow, for $1,500. The shysters didn't know Great-grandfather Chow had … paid off the $1,700 real estate loan and had recorded it at the City's Recorder Office.

Great-grandmother Ning Shee was unable to write in Chinese or English, at the request of the loan shark, Richard B. Bell and S. E. Herrick made some scratch-like marks on the papers handed to her. Great-grandmother Ning Shee did not realize that she was encumbering a lien on the property.

With no experience in handwriting, Great-grandmother Ning Shee made two unusual three-stroke marks on the City Hall records. One three-stroke mark was sort of like a tiny black human figure with arms and legs apart, and the second three strokes represented the Chinese character down.

The three-stroke Chinese character down has the same sound, ha, our nine-stroke family name in China. In Chinese, the terms down and summer are antonyms with the same sounds but different characters and meanings.

As recorded by C. E. Herrick, Tr., to E.J, November 5, 1935, Liber 2757, page 183, there was a default in payment for a loan of $350 at 10 percent per annum on June 6, 1935, in the office of the County Recorder of the City and County of San Francisco, four months after Great-grandmother Ning made the $350 loan. Liber 1789, page 316, recorded the selling of 1016 Washington, November 4, 1935, at the office of C. E. Herrick, 170 Sutter Street, 1935, for $367.76—Carl L. Maritzen was the Notary Public.

The loan shark and real-estate dealer had already sold 1016 Washington to Mr. and Mrs. B, who lived at the Clay-Jones penthouse apartment; Mr. B was assistant Superintendent of Rexall Owl Drug Stores. Mrs. B wanted me to quit school and become a housekeeper for her, and Great-grandmother Ning Shee agreed to Mrs. B's proposal that I become an indentured slave in an effort to get her to return our property. I was still in my early teens and middle school; Mrs. B bought me a black dress with a white half-apron so that I would look more like a maid. Mrs. B showed me how sparkling clean and shiny she wanted her bathrooms, but having lived in Chinatown Mrs. B instructed her elderly Eurasian housekeeper to teach me the ways of a good and proper maid; I was to learn how to be a kitchen helper, such as how to make rice-and-round butter balls for her toast. To make butter balls, a block of butter was cut into half-inch squares and rolled between ping-pong-like paddles. The two paddles were etched with grid-like designs; as one rolled the chunk of butter between the paddles, the grids gave the butter a golf-ball-like design, along with rounding it.

The housekeeper was one of the unwanted offspring of a White John and a prostitute from a Chinatown house of prostitution. At six years of age, she was assigned to a White family by Supervisor Farwell during the 1880s to become a housekeeper for them. The housekeeper gave me her address on John Street, a one-block alley, and told me to see her at her home. She did not want Mrs. B to hear her advising me to go back to school, rather than work as an uneducated housekeeper for White folks like she did.

She was one of the original Joke Sings, being neither pure White nor Chinese in cultural heritage. Supervisor Farwell classified her as one of the contaminants of White man's blood because of her genotype, and therefore racially Chinese only, but in phenotype, she appeared Caucasoid with grey-green eyes and chestnut brown hair.

The housekeeper was married to a retired Chinese house-boy who supplemented their family income by collecting *dirty clothes from White families for several Chinese laundries; he earned a commission from the amount of wash he collected. They also owned the small, two-story wood-frame John Street house for which they paid $900 cash a few years earlier. The housekeeper was afraid to accompany me to speak to my school principal but she did advise me how to explain that she was afraid … but she did tell me how to explain to the school officials why I'd been absent … for almost a month. The Principal sent a truant officer to talk to Great-grandmother Ning.*

The truant officer was a very nice person; he kept smiling and assured me and my mother that we would not be punished for my truancy. My homeroom teacher also came a couple of times during the semester and reminded Great-grandmother Ning that it was illegal to take me out of school to work as a housemaid.

As the story goes, Lennie's mother Ning Shee was outraged that her daughter would defy her wishes, not to mention the loss of income. But Lennie was strong-willed and argued back tenaciously. They bickered constantly for years. Lennie looked for a way out, but by then, a sixteen-year-old Chinese girl had no prospects and was probably in danger of being preyed upon by Tong gangsters. A struggle ensued to pay off the loan shark.

Lennie explains how the account was settled. She writes,

Grandfather Chow had to borrow money from Morris Plan to pay all the fees to regain his own property from the Bergs. In Volume 2924, pg. 118-119, Northern Cos. Title Ins. Co. Tr., March 9, 1936, it is indicated that 1016 Washington was re-recorded back to Chow Chong and Wife at the request of Northern Cos. T. I. Co.

For ten years, Great-grandmother Ning made $28 monthly payments for her loan shark fiasco. Great-grandmother Ning Shee lived at 1016 Washington for the rest of her life.

CHAPTER 18
Rags to Riches

L K Lennie Lee looked for a way out, but those days, a sixteen-year-old Chinese girl had no prospects. She did eventually find a solution. Besides being highly intelligent and forward-thinking, she was quite beautiful. She found work at the 1939 World's Fair working as a hostess. Her job was to wear exotic dresses, pose with tourists, and hand out little favors at the Chinese Pavilion. With the money made from tips, she contributed to household expenses.

LENNIE AS HOSTESS AT THE 1939 INTERNATIONAL EXPOSITION
Family archives.

HERB CAEN

Photo by Nancy Wong, courtesy of Wikimedia Commons.

An iconic columnist for the San Francisco Chronicle, Herb Caen wrote a daily column called *Baghdad by the Bay*. He wrote it for almost sixty years and it was extremely popular. A chance meeting between them early in his career was a portent to their mutual success. One of his earliest assignments was covering the 1939 International Exposition at Treasure Island in the middle of San Francisco Bay.

This is what happened, when she was a young teenager who found work. According to L K Lennie Lee, the job required her to

> *Stand in front of the replica of a Chinese Pagoda, wearing a pretty orange and gold colored velvet floor length Cheong Sarm, high collar Chinese dress. My job was to let tourists take pictures of me and pass out joss sticks and incense, as people came into the Taoist Temple. At the back of the Pagoda was a large ornate shrine with several Chinese gods.*

One day, Herb Caen showed up at the fair ... the problem was that Mr. Ong, the person in charge, did not speak English. ... He had hired someone to lecture in English about the Chinese gods and to instruct tourists to light the joss sticks.

Caen asked Mr. Ong if anything newsworthy had happened ... for his newspaper column. ... As the only person around who spoke English, Mr. Ong solicited me to talk to him about the gods; my knowledge about ... gods was limited. I've seen statues of well-known gods and goddesses, Kwong Kung and Kwan Ying, at the Kwong Chow Temple on Pine Street. That's where I've accompanied Great-grandmother Ning Shee to worship, and I've also seen props of the two gods in Chinatown's operas. The rest of the gods that were lined up behind the shrine, I did not know. Therefore, I told him stories I heard in Chinese school about Ma Lou Jing, or the Monkey God, ... and the rest ... including a Pig God.

I told Herb Caen the Ma Lou Jing story ... as my Chinese school evening class teacher had been spending the last ten to fifteen minutes of class telling us ... a continued-daily story about the Monkey God as a reward. This was a Chinese fairy tale, told from parents to children for many centuries, like the Grimms fairy tales.

For my mother, working at the fair turned out to be a life-changing experience. Her popularity grew after Herb Caen's coverage where she garnered many tips from giving talks and handing out favors to visitors at the Chinese Pavilion.

Besides making several dollars a day during a time when the average wage was .45 cents per hour, Lennie gained self-confidence from making presentations. Thus, she was able to assist with family expenses which improved her relationship with her mother. She carried her newly found assertiveness and self-confidence throughout the rest of her life and it served her well.

L K LENNIE LEE AT SIXTEEN
Family archives.

CHAPTER 19
When Harry Met Lennie

HARRY'S STORY

"What is 'pop's' real name?" An odd question for a young man to ask his mother about his father. Besides Pops, I had always known him as Harry Pang Lee. Lennie's response was Lee Jing Loy, making a cryptic remark: "You are lucky. You are really a Lee, so you don't have to change your name." She then told me that the Wong family, who operated a laundry on Washington Street, were cousins, even though to me they were family friends.

At the time, my parents lived in the Richmond District. From them I learned that a family who had a delicatessen on Clement

MR. AND MRS. LEE
Family archives.

127

Street and operated a nearby restaurant where we often ate were actually close relatives, although we never acknowledged them. As odd as it might seem, these kinds of queries have been asked countless times by generations of descendants wanting to know if Harry was a Paper Son. It is a phenomenon that numerous scholars and historians have written about.

With just a few exceptions, the Chinese Exclusion Act of 1882, and subsequent renewals, barred Chinese immigration and called for deportation. Because of the enormous contributions made by merchants to the overall economy, an exception was made for merchants and their families.

The exclusion laws were somewhat effective until the 1906 earthquake and fire occurred, when most official records at City Hall were destroyed. Everyone was required to update their information. Many Chinese, upon reporting, took the opportunity to claim they had families in China, including sons that did not exist. Virtually no daughters were reported. These fabricated identities created a lucrative enterprise, as these papers were sold to those who wanted to get to America for prices that could reach thousands of dollars.

The below document lists my dad's name as Lee Hing Pang and his father as Lee Fook Chew, who is likely from the same village of Dit Houn Low, Iron Stove Mountain, since recalling facts would be easier.

Harry passed his interview without incident and got his identity card. In case they were stopped by authorities, Chinese persons

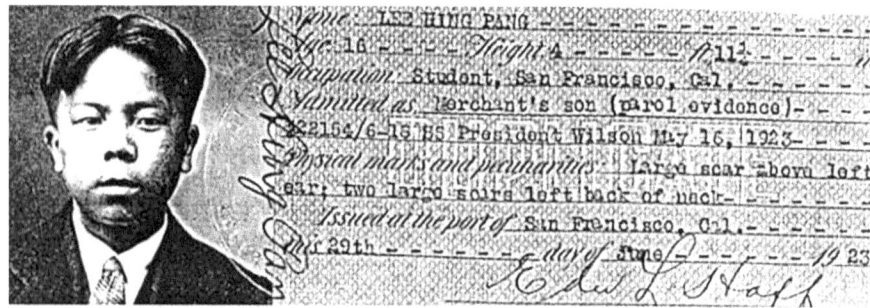

HARRY PANG LEE, PAPER SON

Family archives.

needed to carry identification papers, as they were required to prove their right to remain and that they were not subject to deportation.

Out of fear of discovery, daughters lived quiet lives mostly in Chinatown. Kudos to them from those of us who are from succeeding generations.

Many parents profess they would die for their children. It is the rare individual who is willing to live and spend their entire lives in anonymity for the sake of their progeny. From 1910 to 1943, the end of the Chinese Exclusion Act, and the removal of quotas, countless thousands remained anonymous for their descendants to become Joke Sings.

In 1941, Lennie met Harry, who was working as a bartender. He was fifteen years older than Lennie. They married and Lennie soon had a son at the age of eighteen. Another son followed three years later—that was me. One might think that the future meant a life of drudgery, saddled with two kids at the height of World War II, instead, theirs was an ideal marriage.

CHAPTER 20
Becoming Mrs. Lee

Harry Lee was a very kind man who treated Lennie well. What turned out to be a boon was the fact that Lennie was an ABC—American-born Chinese—and he was a Paper Son who admired and respected her. Contrary to the chauvinistic way most Asian men treated their wives, Harry deferred to her wishes and opinions, which supported her as an outspoken and forward-thinking person, albeit Lennie was not always well-received because her personality could be direct and aggressive. This was against conventional views of Chinese women, and how all women should behave, but Harry cheered on Lennie to dream big and be herself.

For a while Lennie worked as a department store clerk during and after the war, plus waitressing on weekends. A bit of a reconciliation occurred between Lennie and her mother. Ning Shee was happy to watch the two youngsters.

Thanks to the kindness of some relatives who were better off, the young family moved into a comfortable apartment on Clay Street. Ironically, their apartment was located on Nob Hill, just one block from where Ning Yung originally established his holding cemetery. It was a one-bedroom unit that Lennie partitioned into a two-bedroom apartment. She did all the carpentry herself.

Our family lived there for sixteen years, and I thought I was lucky. The majority of my friends lived in Chinatown tenements that had shared kitchens and bathrooms. Technically single-room occupancy or SRO units were designed for one person, but I recall families of eight or more living in them.

Lennie realized the thing she needed to succeed was education. In the early 1950s, nearing the age of thirty, she enrolled at Drew School, a private educational institution that supported students to learn at their own pace. She excelled, earning first a high school diploma, then a Bachelor of Arts from the University of California, Berkeley, and finally a master's degree from the University of San Francisco. Her message to those around her was that education was the way up and out.

Another advantage was that she did not start her career until she was older, so she was never a young, new vulnerable new teacher often assigned to those who are hard to handle. On the other hand, her outspoken, confrontational nature, when she thought something was wrong, made her a thorn in the side to school administrators all the way up to the central office.

In the early 1970s, Lennie became a counselor at Lowell High School. This was, and still is, the academic flagship school for San Francisco. The best students enrolled there. Admission was by test. That standard was changed because many other factors affect academic performance. Location-wise, it was good for commuting from the Richmond District.

Lowell is a notorious school, depending on perspective, for having a very large percentage of Asian American students. Many might assume it is a Mecca for a Model Minority, with hard-working, perfectly behaved students. It was not without issues, however. One situation involved something Lennie had observed back in the 1930s and before, but not as recently as the 70s—polygamy.

Lennie recalled those days, with stories reflecting the times. She spoke about the lessons learned from her students.

In the early 1970s at Lowell High, one of my students from Hong Kong asked for help. She was concerned about losing her home. Her mother was Concubine #7 of a wealthy Hong Kong hotel magnate and she had purchased a home at the Stonestown Shopping Mall neighborhood with money given to her by old man Park before he died.

Old-man Park's grown children from a higher pecking order of concubines 1-6 demanded that Tip-See #7 turn the property over to them. Since the money was old-man Park's, and rightfully theirs by hierarchical polygamous family rules, they possession of it.

Tip See #7 admitted that she was from a poor family and that she had become old-man Park's concubine to improve her living conditions. A few months after old-man Park died, friends and relatives helped her flee to the United States with her two young children, and took the money and jewelry old-man Park had given her.

My advice to my student's mother, her all-female friends, and relatives, who also came to see me at Lowell, was to ignore the other Tip Sees adult children since her daughter would soon graduate from Lowell and her older son was already working at Metropolitan Life Insurance Company. They already have their green cards, and they would soon become American citizens.

Hopefully, things worked out for the family Lennie described. For her, the incident was an example of the high regard her students had for her and a reminder that the use of concubines still existed, even in the ostensibly progressive 1970s.

Tragically, there was another scenario that was worse than becoming a concubine. Lennie changed assignments in 1979 and went to Galileo High School across town. That school wasn't a plum assignment. Amongst other things, it was a notorious incubator of Chinatown gang activity. An outspoken critic of school administrators and their lack of understanding, it the transfer likely occurred to move her away from the pleasant assignment at Lowell.

Again, Asian students developed a high respect for L K Lennie Lee and even the gangster types left her alone. Moreover, she allied with African American teachers to improve conditions for everyone. Students opened up to her, and she was reminded that some things do not change or improve over the passage of time.

Lennie spoke about that experience and the change of environments. In her new school assignment,

Some of Galileo High Asian students living in the Tenderloin District had school attendance problems, and sometimes we held class discussions concerning these

problems. The tragic stories told by my high-absentee stu-
dents reminded me of my school classmates.

A couple of students told me about how, at first, their
parents were ... against prostitution. However, when
... a well-dressed madam, came around to recruit them
... with the notion that their daughters could make as
much as $3,000 per week, things changed. A tenth-grade
Cambodian student complained that her parents had ac-
cepted $2,000 from an elderly Asian man in Texas to
be his concubine: her parents made life miserable for her
because they had spent some of the money.

Stories I've heard before when growing up in the ten-
ements of old Chinatown, except I listened to the same
stories as an integrated schoolteacher, teaching among
many White administrators, and those who commuted
from the suburbs and were indifferent toward inner-city
student problems.

These incidents were not only examples of the high regard L K
Lennie Lee's students had for her but also it was a reminder that
exploitation still existed. Thus, there was another scenario that was
worse than becoming a concubine—prostitution. There were good
stories, too whereby former students expressed appreciation of my
mother. I witnessed some of these interactions.

"Hi, Mrs. Lee!" The young Asian waitress was genuinely pleased
to be serving her. *"I'm going to City College full-time!"*

"That's good. I went to 'City' too, before transferring to UC."

The young woman was beaming. Encounters like that happened
on a fairly regular basis.

Invested in her community of upbringing, almost every week-
end, Lennie and Harry returned to Chinatown. They parked in the
Portsmouth Square garage, had dinner at a restaurant, then walked
up the hill to Waverly Place to socialize at the Nam Chung Music
Club. Neither of them played an instrument. It was a social gathering place that was centrally significant to them.

PART IV

CHINATOWN LIFE

L K LENNIE LEE WROTE FIRST-HAND ACCOUNTS OF DAILY LIFE IN CHINATOWN. SHE VIRTUALLY OBSERVED ALL ASPECTS OF LIFE THERE, BOTH THE GOOD, BAD, AND INDIFFERENT. BEYOND DIRECT OBSERVATION, OTHERS ALSO TRUSTED HER WITH THEIR OWN STORIES.

FOR EXAMPLE, SHE RECORDED AN EXTENSIVE ORAL HISTORY OF HER GRANDUNCLE NING CHOIE TANE, WHO WAS BORN IN 1843. HE RELATED STORIES OF LENNIE'S FAMILY, INCLUDING HER GRANDFATHER CHOW TICK LEE, WHO WAS BORN IN YERBA BUENA IN 1833, MAKING HIM ONE THE EARLIEST CHINESE AMERICANS.

ALTHOUGH HER HUSBAND HARRY WAS A PAPER SON, HE HAD A LARGE CIRCLE OF ACQUAINTANCES IN CHINATOWN; HIS EXTENDED FAMILY WAS VERY INVOLVED IN THE CIGAR MANUFACTURING BUSINESS. THERE WERE MANY OTHER MEMORIES, IN WHICH THE NAM CHUNG MUSIC CLUB PLAYED A KEY PART IN L K LENNIE LEE'S RECOVERY OF THEIR HISTORY.

CHAPTER 21
Nam Chung Music Club

Besides holding an extensive collection of Chinese American history books, Lennie tapped into two unique sources of information not available to academic researchers. From the oral histories she collected in conversations with Chinatown residents and relatives, these included granduncle Ning Fook Tane who was born in 1843. She also recorded oral histories from members of the Nam Chung Music Club (NMC, or "South-Center Music Club"). The NMC was an example of how Joke Sings and sojourners socialized. Many ethnic groups formed similar organizations, though their activities may not have been driven by music.

Our family, except for my brother Leonard who had joined the Air Force by then, moved to the Richmond District in 1959. Nonetheless, we continuously returned to Chinatown for almost everything. In some sense, we were modern sojourners. Still, unlike other families, we didn't assimilate into Richmond.

There, my parents participated in social activities with the Nam Chung Music Club, even though neither played a musical instrument. Typically, Lennie gambled in a low-stakes Mahjong game, but her principal activity focused on gossip, while Harry sat in the main room and reminisced about old times.

Sharing about her experiences with the Nam Chung Music Club, Lennie wrote,

> *Most of the Lou How Yun or Left-Behind Chinese in the United States ... were from the south-center Canton province, around the Kwong Hoy Seaport area. The members' ages ranged from mid-teens to late-eighties, a group of about sixty young to elderly lonely single men banded together to form a social-music club ... a place to*

*spend time, socialize, and play Chinese music, naming it
the Nam Chung Music Club and South-Center Music.*

*Anti-Chinese hostile environments ... made it difficult to
find permanent jobs in San Francisco. So, many ... were
forced to leave town to find work, but they wanted a nest,
a home base during holidays such as Chinese New Year,
to be among folks of their own culture in San Francisco.
Because most members would more likely have the day
off annually to celebrate their charter day, in 1924, Nam
Chung Music Club members chose the Fourth of July.*

*Wong See Bo, a root-pioneer elder whom I first met as a
child, while still living at the Suey Ying Tong's headquarters
building, helped the group rent a second-floor apartment at
the Wong Family Association building on Waverly Place.
The Wong Family Building was narrow ... with a ground-
floor barber shop and a street-entry basement.*

*Nam Chung charter members divided the twenty-five
by fifty feet apartment into a front room, a music and
meeting hall, a narrow seven-foot-long kitchen, a toilet
nearby, and three rooms in the middle: one small and two
mid-size, with a false ceiling over one room ... which
was approximately four feet*

*below the original twelve-foot ceiling—the space between
them was for storage. Two of the rooms were social, mahjong, or gambling rooms, and the third small room, once
utilized as a bedroom, became a storage space.*

*Mark Kuen, who owned the Sing Chong Chinese Bazaar
across from the historical Saint Mary's Church at Dupont
and California, was elected first president of the Nam Chung
Music Club. For the many Nam Chung men who didn't
have permanent addresses, a larger-than-normal wooden
mailbox was added to the Wong Building's entryway.*

Great-Grandfather Albert Bew Chan, the ten-year-old messenger boy shown in the Long-Distance Telephone Company's photo entitled "Chinatown's First Switchboard – Circa 1895" was one the 1924 charter members of the Club. Albert Bew Chan's granddaughter, Lucretia Chan, married my son, Ronald Lee. Ronald's father, Lee Jing Loy, my husband, joined the Nam Chung Music Club during the 1930s Christmas holidays.

At the start of 1930, most Nam Chung members were either out of work, out of town looking for work, or employed seasonally in fishing, operating a laundry, or farming. It wouldn't be long before the Nam Chung Music Club was four months behind in rent, and some of the Wong family administrators had placed on their meeting agenda its eviction.

During the heated meeting, Wong Yin Doon listened to his elder Wong See Bo and offered a "No eviction yet!" proposal. The Wongs voted to give the music club more time to find money to pay the rent. Nam Chung's gas and light had been shut off for two months for non-payment of bills, and two homeless elders were living there. Nam Chung officers held a survival technique meeting … where they decided to recruit new members with jobs.

Grand cousin Ngauk Loy, also a charter member, approached Grandfather Jing Loy concerning

Nam Chung's financial predicament and wanted his Clan cousin to join the club and help out. Grandfather Jing Loy did not play any musical instruments or sing, but Grand-cousin Ngauk Loy persuaded him to become a member. He also talked Grandfather Jing Loy into asking his employer, Bimbo's, at 365 Market, to advance him a month's wages to pay Nam Chun's gas and light bills. His employer complied.

Wong Wai was in his early forties, when I first met him at NMC in the 1940s. Wong See Bo persuaded Wong Wai to join. Although he also didn't play music, or sing, like Grandfather Jing Loy he gambled and played mah-jong. Wong Wai and several other members who joined at the same time ... became close friends. Two members who had jobs in the peninsula and two cars between them joined NMC ... That's when a carpool was started ... for non-driving NMC members to commute daily to work at peninsula restaurants.

In time, more NMC members were able to get permanent jobs instead of seasonal work. Sometimes, during days off, they drove to wherever NMC members were just to say "Hello!" The NMC drivers also visited friends along the Monterey Peninsula, where some of them had once found work as fishermen or restaurant cooks. At that time, the fishing business in Monterey ... and canneries along Cannery Row were closed, and Chinatown was quiet.

The drivers and fellow NMC members visited places such as Salinas and Watsonville, where they purchased rights to harvest fruits and vegetables from White farmers. NMC harvesters formed a cooperative to share profits from the gatherings... and peddled the produce all over California and up to the neighboring state of Arizona. NMC drivers and their entourage also visited friends along the Monterey Peninsula, where some had once worked.

Several NMC members, including Grandfather Jing Loy, started a Chinese American restaurant in San Francisco. They opened their businesses ... in the working men's neighborhoods where folks could afford inexpensive food, such as ours in the Tenderloin District.

Chinese dishes usually were a mixture of vegetables, including Bok Choy and Chinese Chard with some sort of meat over rice or noodles. American-style dishes were also served. ... Comparatively less expensive in the Tenderloin, they included hardy meals, such as corned beef and cabbage, ham hock and lima beans, stew, pork chops, fried chicken, and hamburger steak.

World War II was a financially flush era for NMC members. Some found work at the shipyards and hotels. Others purchased or started Pa-and-Ma type of laundry, grocery, restaurant businesses in White only middle-class neighborhoods such as Laurel Village, Pacific Heights, and the Richmond District.

NMC, as a music club, was highly involved with fund-raising activities by the Chinese Relief Association of the United States. Club members traveled the country to stage plays and joined in with Chinatown's parades to help refugees who suffered terribly from Sino-Japan (1937) and World War II wars. NMC members were all men, prior to World War II.

From habits of living in a largely all-male society, where foul language was used even when bantering with each other. At a meeting, the men established rules not to use foul language or allow Chinatown's underworld characters to join the club. With no foul language rules established, NMC men fixed up and decorated the place, bought new furniture, new mahjong games, and instruments, such as the Butterfly Harp and all sorts of new songs and plays. The idea was to attract females to join the music club.

A money pot rule was established as an honor, self-help system, whereby any club member who found himself swearing placed twenty-five cents into the pot. In time, when men stopped swearing, there was no money.

Now female members swear along with the men and also make sexually derogatory statements. From mid-1940 to

1950, NMC members held Tri-city Chinese New Year Celebrations. As two of the largest family Clans in San Francisco, the Lee and Wong co-ops organized the tri-city Chinese New Year celebrations. The tri-cities were San Francisco, Stockton, and Sacramento. With strong brotherly love amongst them, they created historical ties to help each other survive those Anti-coolieism and Yellow Journalism agitation days.

The tri-city Chinese New Year celebrations lasted four-days and three-nights. Hotels were reserved ahead of time. NMC members organized carpools, chartered buses, and rented a truck to bring the musical instruments. For the first day of festivities, they sent colorful costumes to Sacramento. Some female NMC members wore cus-tom-order beautifully beaded, sequenced garments from Hong Kong. They looked beautiful singing in front of a mike, accompanied by members who played musical in-struments, consisting of the butterfly harp, pei-pa, flute, violin, guitar, and gong. There was a continuous series of solo and duet singers.

Those who traveled from afar registered at the Travelers Hotel near the old Lee Family Association and celebrated at several clubs until the wee hours of the morning. Then, the members drove to Stockton …. There, we registered at a hotel that folk had reserved for the group; we socialized, sang, put on skits, gambled, and toured a couple of new homes purchased by NMC members. Like Sacramento, the Stockton folks had loaded several tables with Deem Sum and other delicacies served throughout the day. For dinner, Stockton hosted a banquet meal, which occupied a couple of Chinatown restaurants. Finally, the entou-rage returned to San Francisco for the third festivity and banquet …. There, several NMC men and actor friends wrote a comedy skit and presented it at a Chinatown theatre. The skit was a funny satire, a lampoonery, and a parody about how ... country folks back in China squatted wherever they went.

The skit players performed a hilarious squat act. They spoofed their country-folks dialect and folksy propriety, and the actors were extremely funny and entertaining. The skit climax came to an end when several of the agile actors, with support of increasingly louder music, in unison and in a squatting position, jumped from the floor onto their chairs to eat dinner still squatting.

Traditionally, country folks ... tend to squat whenever they met on the road and carried on a conversation. They also squatted when playing cards and various games in the open and even squatted on their chairs at the dinner table.

Nam Chung Musical Club once had many volunteers ... to decorate, host, shop, cook, wash dishes, and clean up the place. Raymond Lee, a schoolmate at Francisco Jr. High, was a longtime unofficial ... artistic and elaborate decorator. For Christmas, he usually purchased a floor-to-ceiling tree and rented movies for the children. Food was served buffet-style because there were usually fifty to seventy hungry folks hanging around to eat.

A number of out-of-town NMC members showed up several times a year, and Arizona's state senator Wing F. Ong, who loved to sing and improvise Chinese homespun, wove his country-folk blue-storytelling songs. The senator and other singers launched into spontaneous songs and sang unpretentiously for hours. Some of the songs were similar to southern country-folk music, accompanied with two to four-string musical instruments such as the guitar, banjo, violin, and fiddle.

Wing Ong known for highlighting music threw in a few loud and clear jokingly sarcastic remarks about how poor the group once was, the harsh lifestyle they lived during their youth, and the trickery young men resorted to, to filch food to eat. One song was about how they extended their pant pockets to pick more fruits from the farmers' trees, as they sneaked into orchards. Soon, their pockets were so heavily laden ... that they had problems keeping up their pants.

Another improvised song was about how the Ongs, as a poor out of work couple during the Great Depression and as young entrepreneurs, loaded an old flat truck with free cantaloupes which California farmers couldn't sell. They drove up and down the old roads and under the hot sun of Arizona and sold their cantaloupes—that's how they settled in Phoenix and started their grocery business.

During a conversation with State Senator Wing Ong, I brought up ... The Bay Guardian, *March 28, 1972, news article entitled "Meanwhile, back in Chinatown," which featured a picture of my nephew, Herbert Kenneth, as one of San Francisco State University's lead protesters.*

I quoted some statements made by The Guardian *writers concerning Wong Yin Doon. I compared them to Yin Doon's historical relationship with Nam Chung Music Club's survival during the Great Depression. I brought up the article up because Senator Wing Ong had said ... that Chiang Kai-shek also invited him to attend some of Taiwan's national meetings, and he met Wong Yin Doon there.*

Like Wong Yin Doon, Wing Ong was also Hoy Sun heritage by birth. Hoy Sun folks have the largest number of Hoy Sun district associations in America. This was one of the major reasons Taiwan politicians were interested in getting them involved with or supporting their government. ...Chiang Kai-shek invited Wing because he was a businessman, an attorney, an Arizona state senator, and a well-known longtime officer of a number of Phoenix Chinatown organizations and the Ong Family Clan Association.

Wing Ong and I were once sort of fellow penny-ante gamblers. We played the games called Da Gai, Hit the Chicken, Sub Sarm Jang, and Thirteen Cards. In the Da Gai game, we used six small dice and threw them into a porcelain bowl. The way the numbers came up determined how one wins. Sub Sarm Jang was similar to Pai Gow Poker played in Reno and Las Vegas, except thirteen cards were used instead of seven. Wing's wife, Rose, who was nicknamed Jong See Mo, or Lawyer's Wife played the two dollar a thousand-points mahjong with us. It was an old-style game, played much slower and largely for social purposes. The amiable social get-together-styled game has largely been eliminated at the club.

At the time, I also quit going to NMC for several years to transfer to UC Berkeley where I was on my fourth year of foreign language requirements in a French class at City College where the professor administered a surprise quiz on Monday, and I received an "F." Two days before Monday, I played mahjong on Saturday and Sunday and did not study; it was a good thing this happened in the beginning of the semester, and I had time to make up the grade before finals.

Just like Paul Robeson, the actor, who sang about the Black slave toilers at the Mississippi River, the NMC men sang about the harshness of living as China river-boat-toilers. These toilers, with strong hemp rope, had to pull cargo-loaded river boats up the river to the upland of China.

During the 1970s, some of the new NMC members were from Hong Kong, who played music from notes and tended to ridicule old-timers for their improvised folk country music. With the loss of merriment and comradeship, many of the NMC's old-timers stopped coming and quit the club.

Loss of memberships also meant no revenues, such as Heung Yow or Incense and Oil donations to support the club. A number of the NMC old-timers passed away; some moved to the Richmond District, and others to the Sunset District or out of town. Sister-in-law Janet, who is still a member of Nam Chung Club, told me ... membership had declined seriously, and expressed that the music club would soon be gone.

At the end of the 1940s, Chinese American WWII veterans finally won their case to move into segregated neighborhoods, which included the Richmond District. Soon, White Flight began, leaving many Clement Street business stores empty, and there was not even one Chinese business when I moved into the Richmond District in 1958.

At our 8th Avenue and Cabrillo property in 1964, many of the old historical houses in my neighborhood were sold for ten to twelve thousand dollars. Many of the old houses were purchased by Chinese, and a significant number by NMC members. Store buildings at Clement were offered ... for thirty to forty thousand dollars and were largely purchased by Chinese Americans. Richmond District soon was called the New Chinatown.

The Hong Kong Styled Mahjong Game, introduced a couple of decades ago, was foreign to me. It was a much more intense and faster game with higher stakes, and it eliminated the cumbersome procedures of counting points to win. Some of the new immigrant men, usually with a lighted cigarette in one hand, favored bashing *the hard mahjong tiles onto the wooden table, creating a loud-sharp noise, mouthing hullabaloo to emphasize the tile they were about to throw out into the middle of the table. They also played at pretty high stakes, not the two-thousand-dollar points of the old-fashioned game. By the mid-1950s, NMC had saved $20,000 dollars in the bank, and during the early 1960s, the three-story red brick building with a restaurant across Waverly Street was for sale for $40,000. Surprisingly, Mark Kuen, NMC's charter member president, and several peers adamantly refused to okay the building purchase.*

When queried about the purchase, they replied that the haughty newcomer urbanite members from Hong Kong had changed the initial concept of the formation of the Nam Chung Music Club in 1924, which focused on volunteerism and mutual aid to survive in a hostile society. They predicted that the haughty, better educated, newcomer urbanites, who had never suffered White racism, with their derogatory and snickering remarks concerning the lesser educated old timers, would cause disunity and permanent clique problems between old and new NMC members.

In 1996, NMC still had the $20,000 in the bank, which the old-time members had long kept as a reserve, not allowing the new members to touch it. Thus, some new members splintered off from NMC and formed their own musical club.

The purchasing power of the $20,000 went down substantially in the last three decades of inflation. The market price of the three-story red brick building across the street is now worth millions.

CHAPTER 22
Chinatown: A Multicultural Place

Virtually every historian's description of early Chinatown life describes a Bachelor Society. The photo below is often cited as an example. Historian Charlie Chin of the Chinese Historical Society of America perceived bachelor societies as:

> Made up of men who were bachelor's only in the sense that they were here by themselves because of the law. They all had wives and children in China who could not join them. This lasted well into the early '60s. As late as the '70s, old Toishan uncles were still living in an apartment where they had been for twenty, thirty, or forty years, from the day when they first arrived and became trapped in time. The

BACHELOR COMMUNITY
Courtesy of Wikipedia Commons.

148

People's Republic of China had been founded; there was no way for them to get back home … and they had lost touch with their families. They had been set adrift, cut off, because there was no way for them to return. The world that they knew was gone.

Most descriptions give the impression that the enclave was a monolithic place. However, for Lennie, Chinatown was a multicultural place. In her quest to share its complexity and make up, she wrote about ethnic neighborhoods around Chinatown.

Chinatown's street and business names were not necessarily Romanized phonetically in English, and cultural, race or community names were used instead. Great-Great-Granduncle Choie Tane rented the store for his cargo re-addressing and re-forwarding his agency business as Far Yuen Got Gai, or Garden Corner Street Brenham Place. Waverly Place was named Tin How Mui Gai, meaning Sky God Temple Street. Ross Alley was named Now Lo Soun Hong, meaning Old Spanish or Mexican Alley. It was said that during the Yerba Buena days many Mexicans who spoke Spanish lived in Ross Alley. Spofford Alley was named Sun Lo Sown Hong, meaning New Spanish Alley. Also, many Filipinos who spoke Spanish settled among the Chinese … in Spofford Alley.

She also wrote about the presence of African Americans in Portsmouth Square. Lennie recalled,

Ning Choie Tane rented a store, 11 Brenham Place, across the street from Far Yuen, Garden, Portsmouth Square. Though his business was known as the Canton Company among the Chinese, White truckers called it the Chinatown Branch of the Wells Fargo Express Company because he continued to use that business to deliver cargo and mail.

149

The store was not very large. Across the rear, he built an eight-foot-wide loft and partitioned the underside into a small room and used it as his living quarters, while the loft stored cargo. Wooden crates from China were sent to the wharf, and he carted them from the wharf to his store to properly re-address in English and forward it to other parts of the country.

As a child, I used to help Granduncle Choie Tane re-stamp addresses in English. I hung up the approximately fourteen by eighteen inches diamond-shaped, bright red and green backdrop Wells Fargo Drayage Company sign on the Shing Chong building next door so that the White truck drivers could see the sign and know where to stop to pick up the cargo.

The store was on the ground floor of the Suey Ying Tong Headquarters building where I was born. His younger brother, Granduncle Ning Fook Tane, went to work for a Ning Clan uncle who had a shrimp fishing business at Ha Liu Chune, Shrimp Products Village, Mission Creek. Ha Liu Chune was an old Chinese fishing or shrimping village specializing in catching and drying bay shrimps to be exported, which was said to have existed in Yerba Buena for more than a hundred years before it was re-named San Francisco.

Two homeless African Americans did piece work for the drainage agency; they helped load and unload the cargo and got paid only when there was work. At night, they slept on top of the cargo in the store or in the loft. When daylight came, they washed up at the Portsmouth Square bathroom facilities. It was a hangout for African Americans who hoped to get day jobs, such as being hired by moving companies. The African Americans who lived in Chinatown were not starving; like the Chinese, they ate animal entrails or chitterlings, which the Whites wouldn't eat.

Granduncle Choie Tane usually got entrails free. For a few cents per pound from Rose's, the meat market of my Sister-in-Law's father, Hop Sang Meat Market, as well as from a couple of Chinatown meat markets, which he shared with his Black friends. Chinese called chitterlings Ngow Job, meaning Beef Entrails; The Ngow Job also contained entrails of other animals, such as pigs and chicken, and are still served at most Dim Sum restaurants today.

Lennie discussed the origin of Ngow Job as a foodstuff Chinese and African Americans shared in common. By way of an example, she wrote a Chinese legend.

An emperor traveling in disguise found out that his citizens were suffering from hunger. Thus, he commanded butchers to kill the cows and cook them for the starved citizens. The king hoped every citizen could eat it. So besides cooking the beef, the entrails of cows were also put into the pot to cook more. Citizens thought the dish tasted good, and it passed on from generation to generation.

On the next page, a group of Black residents are pictured on Clay Street west of Stockton Street. Unfortunately, fire engulfed their homes. To their right, across the way, would be Joice Street, where Chow Chong's family later rented a flat.

Lennie continued her narrative, providing a perspective of the environment in which they lived.

An Afro-American church was at the corner of Powell and John Street. Reverend William Cooper Sr. was the Minister. Helen Cooper, a fellow Afro-American Latin teacher at Lowell, was married to Reverend William Cooper Jr., the son of the Minister.

From the library, Helen Cooper helped me find the California Historical Society text, which had a statement concerning Great-Great-Great-Granduncle Ning Yung. In a small semi-basement storefront next door to the Hop Sang Meat Market on Pacific Avenue was Father Devine's Black Muslim Church. ... The church was known for its large bowls of fruit placed on the tables, which one could see from the open doorway. Father Devine's followers were known as "Angels." He and his Angels encouraged my siblings and me to help ourselves with the goodies.

One time, we children collected whatever money we had and donated sixteen cents to the offering box, and listened

AFRICAN AMERICANS WHO LIVED NEAR CHINATOWN, 1906
Photo by Arnold Genthe, courtesy of Fine Arts Museums of San Francisco.

to him preach. The Afro-American church, I believed, was sold after World War II and became Chinatown's only mortuary for four decades; it was operated by Whites.

The two Chinese-operated funeral houses, Wing Sang and Quong Fook Sang were closed during the 1960s. The historic old Black church building, which was converted into the Cathay Mortuary, was torn down, and was replaced by a small neighborhood city park. Cathay Mortuary, the last funeral house in old Chinatown, was moved to the Richmond District, at 9th and Geary.

In her writings, Lennie recorded Chinese community life, documented cultural and foodstuff practices, as well as the organization of work, and employment. Cigar and sewing factories were also part of her narrative.

CHAPTER 23
Narm Bo Mo Bay Khoun—Sewing Factories

Lennie wrote about the sewing factory, recalling the part it played in their lives, its organization and distribution of labor, along with its damage to workers. She recalled,

> *After school, my duty was to go straight to the sewing factory to get instructions on how to shop for the family dinner before going to Chinese school at 5 p.m.—Chinese school was 5 to 8 p.m. daily and 9 to 12 on Saturday.*

> *The Powell Street sewing factory, where my mother worked specialized in inexpensive floral-printed cotton dresses. It was classified as a Far Bo Gai Chong or Floral Cloth Sewing Factory.*

BLUE LINT NOSTRILS
Family archives.

White contractors restricted the type of sewing subcontractors could make in their factories. Some factories specialized in finer work, such as silk and social dresses. They were classified as a See Far Gai Chong or Silk Sewing Factory.

The third factory's classification was the Louie Jai Fu Gai Chong, or Laborer Pants Sewing Factory. (Jade Snow Wong's family business would have been in this category.) Louie Jai Fu or Laborer Pants referred to those who wore blue jeans, overalls, and coveralls.

Laborer Pants were larger than nowadays because men usually wore them over their street clothes while at work. Color and texture of denim blue jeans which are sold at department stores today are also not the same as the dark blue jeans of the old days; the dark blue coloring used to come off, and the materials were very coarse, therefore the restrictions from other types of sewing in the same factory by White contractors. In the old days, blue denim jeans were worn by men only; today, they are also made smaller, in various styles, and worn by women, children, and the elderly.

The sewing factories were also classified by the seamstresses according to the skill requirements, the type of sewing machine, the materials used, and the working conditions. Silk materials required fine handling and the most sewing experience. See Fat Gai Chong paid the seamstresses by the dress. The dress buyers paid the most and were the most selective. The Far Bo Gai Chong seamstresses were paid by the dozens. These were the less expensive dresses.

At the bottom level was the Laborers' Sewing Factories, in which the seamstresses sewed blue jeans, which the color also came off via the moisture in their hands. Sewing blue jeans was rough work. Besides the blue coloring, which tended to stain the seamstress' hands, materials left blue lint all over the place, including the seamstress's hair, clothing, and floor, besides Narm Bo Mo, or Blue Lint, in their nostrils.

Breathing in Narm Bo Mo was a health hazard that could have caused tuberculosis (TB) among the seamstresses, thus my teacher in high school encouraged me to find other work. In the 1930s, the health department had a tuberculosis test program at the schools, and Chinatown children tested positive most; I tested positive. The school nurse told me I would always test positive with TB serum tests. Therefore, I should only take chest X-rays.

As a schoolteacher, for fifty years, I have taken many chest x-rays, … required every two years. Then, my physician suggested take the tuberculin serum skin tests because some of the readings could've been false positive. I tested negative.

Piecework sewing was not steady work. The seamstresses worked long hours and took home work when it was available. Sometimes, there was no work for weeks. The dress materials came to the Powell Street sewing factory cut out in six-to-ten-inch-thick stacks of paper.

A finished dress was sent as a pattern Lau Mae Shee, the proprietress, who separated the cut material into groups following the patterns. The seamstresses completed the dress. There were no written instructions since most of the women were illiterate. Sometimes, if Great-Grandmother Ning Shee liked the dress style … she traced the pattern in newspaper. Then, we would go to downtown department stores to buy inexpensive yardage remnants.

Until the 1960s, all downtown department stores had a home yardage department. Sometimes, we would find two or three-yard pieces of pretty odd-and-end materials for as low as twenty-five cents for each remnant.

At age ten, I was anxious to earn money at the sewing factory to make my dresses from remnant materials. By the time I was twelve, I was making my own dresses. The main reason ... I made my own dresses was because Great-Grandmother Ning Shee, being a thrifty person, tended to make them loose and down to the ankles. To save money, she made them at least two sizes larger than the size I wore.

In the 1940s, I worked at the Emporium. When fur-collared coats were on sale, I decided to buy her one. Great-Grandmother Ning Shee insisted upon getting a garment that was two sizes larger for her, ... she wanted extra material ... when she needed them. Another time, when I was buying her a dress, she argued, "A larger dress costs the same as a smaller one, and also, I may need to wear several layers of clothing underneath if it gets cold."

We collected all sorts of shapes, sizes, and colors of buttons and multi-colored left-over threads from sewing factories to use. Seamstresses were collectors of leftover materials, and they exchanged ... whatever materials they had accumulated. I inherited Great-Grandmother Ning Shee's sewing-day collections, including her commercial Singer Sewing Machine. During the 70s, I donated it to a needy organization, but I still have some of her sewing material collections. In fact, many of the old buttons were in good condition, prettier, and of better quality than those sold nowadays.

When I was seven, I started working in the sewing factories during summer vacations, school holidays, and weekends. These workplaces were a social outlet for many of the seamstresses. At break times for lunch or snacks many stories and gossip was told when they got together.

One Saturday, while having lunch together, we discussed Dai Gat Paw, Big Feet Women, and the advantages of not having bounded feet in America. Most of the women who worked in Lau Mae Shee's sewing factory were Dai Gat Pat, whose normal size feet had never been bound.

Great-grandmother Ning Shee was classified as a Fong Gat Paw, Unbounded Feet Woman, even though Great-grandmother Ning's feet were once bounded as a six-year-old child and unbounded a few months later when China's anti-Ching Dynasty revolutionists came out against the binding of women's feet. Both Great-Grandmother Ning's and her older sister's feet were bound for a few months by their grandmother until their father gave the firm and final order to "Stop it!" He insisted that the binding of feet was a past practice. Great-Grandmother Ning's father also refused to drown his second daughter, Great-Grandmother Ning Shee, as an infant.

Great-Grandmother Ning was a Ma Nui, Mother's Daughter, and was not a Mui Nui, or Slave Girl, even though her family was poor. Lau Mae Shee's mother, an elderly widow, was the only Jod Gat Paw, or Bounded Feet Woman in the place. She was the family's babysitter and the factory's rice cooker. She envied the women who never had their feet bound and could go shopping downtown. The forepart of her foot was bent under, force-folded to the heels with white strips of cloth. She sometimes took off the strips to allow her feet to air for a while.

Besides having deformed, stunted feet that were substantially impossible to walk on, her feet bothered her constantly. She had to soak and oil them almost every day. She considered herself blessed to have a daughter and daughter-in-law who were willing to trim and cut her toenails since she couldn't do it herself and did not have goun yun or servants.

Chinese men in the U.S. preferred Dai Gat Paw as wives because they were needed as helpmates, especially in families operating labor-intensive type of businesses like laundries and Chop Suey houses.

YOUNG GIRL WITH BOUND FEET
Courtesy of Wikipedia Commons.

I've never seen or heard of an American-born Chinese woman who ever had her feet bound. Bounded feet were for women of leisure who didn't need to work or attend school away from home. Bounding of little girls' feet also did not become a custom because Chinatown's children, including girls, were a large part of the child-labor force for family survival.

In the old days in China, Jod Gat Paw were considered women of leisure and usually had a few personal servants who took care of their needs. Dai Gat Paw were lower class women, usually servants, slaves, farm workers or wives of the poor.

The bounded-feet custom and elaborate clothing of ancient China was sort of like European elite of the Marie

Antoinette era when the men and women of wealth fashioned elaborate wigs, wore makeup, and extraordinary clothing. Men used make-up and wore brocade clothing, jewelry, and tight silk stockings. Women wore tight waist-cinching underwear to achieve a small waistline, along with wire-shaped dresses with huge, uncomfortable bustles.

Besides bound feet and elaborately embroidered clothing, Chinese women wore wigs with elaborate trinkets and jewelry adornments. Men also wore silk Cheun Po, and Long Clothing, or long-skirted clothing and grew long fingernails to show they were men of leisure and wealth.

As class recognition, the rulers restricted the peasants from wearing colorful clothing. Among the emperors, lesser rulers, and princes, the color of clothing, ornaments, and decorations showed their ruling power. Yellow was for the emperors only, and red was for the lesser rulers. By imperial doctrine, peasants were forbidden to wear colorful clothing.

During the 1930s, I never saw young women with bound feet walking around Chinatown; there were several older women with bound feet. No Chinese women with bound feet were visible due to the 1924 exclusion law forbidding wives of American Chinese to immigrate to the U.S.

Once in a while, when the weather was sunny-warm, one or two Chinatown's elderly Bounded Feet Women ventured out to be seen in Far Yuen or walking along Dupont Gai, as all the east-to-west paralleled streets in Chinatown were steep hills and hard for Jod Gat Paw to climb.

Great-Grandfather Chow Chong bought an Indentured Slave Girl for Grandmother June Chow; the Indentured Slave Girl got married at nineteen, right before Grandmother left for America in 1920.

There's a difference between Indentured Slaves and Sai Doy, or Forever Boy. Indentured slaves worked for a designated period and had the right to marry or get their freedom. Much like Indentured Chinese Slaves, Whites … brought them to America during the gold rush and railroad-building days. Sai Doy were like the American blacks because their descendants or children were also born slaves.

I first learned about Sai Doy when Great-Grandmother Ning Shee inquired about Grandfather Lee's family background in relation to the Lee Cigar Manufacturing Business. Apparently, several of the men who worked at the Lee cigar business during the period between 1870s-1900s were runaways. Two of the seamstresses were once sold as Indentured Slave Girls by their pauperized parents, with the right for them to get married once they became adults.

Once in a while, Indentured Slave Girls spoke about their harsh lives. One former seamstress, Wong Lei Shee, spoke about her life as a slave girl from ten to sixteen years of age. At 5'7" and 150 pounds, she was tall and husky for a Chinese woman of those days. She was already a tall child at ten when sold. At sixteen, her cousin in America found her a middle age Gum San Hock, Gold Mountain Man. Gum San Hock was a widowed dishwasher; he was a thrifty, hardworking, non-gambling and kind man. He paid the slave-master $200 dollars to buy her freedom so that she could travel to America and marry him.

Her poverty-stricken parents sold her … for $50 dollars. Her task was to be a companion playmate to a whining, whimpering, asthmatic spoiled brat whom she nicknamed Lon Chone, or Lazy Worm. He was the slave master's only son and four years younger than her.

Walking was the major mode of transportation in Wong Lei Shee's remote village high up in the Hoy Sun Mountains. Lon Chone didn't like to walk and used his poor health as an excuse to demand that Wong Lei Shee serve as his personal Leon Gat Chair, Two-legged Car. Lon Choun rode piggyback on Wong Lei Shee on winding roads up and down the hills to and from his school each day. Six years later, she was still Lon Choun's Leon Gat Chair. Of slight build, he was already twelve years of age. He became irritated instead of considerate when Wong Lei Shee stopped and rested.

Meanwhile, Wong Lei Shee complained to her parents about the predicament they had put her in when they sold her into slavery. Her parents wrote to her cousin in America to find a husband for their daughter. That was how at sixteen she married a husband twenty-five years older. She gained an understanding stepson who was five years older than her and had a ten-year-old daughter of her own.

A second seamstress talked about her husband, who couldn't find work in San Francisco and went to Houston, Texas, to work as a cook on a cattle ranch. She hoped to see him in a few months. Her husband was trying to get her to work as a live-in cleaning woman or babysitter so they could be closer to each other; he had borrowed money from a loan shark to bring her to America. To pay off the debt of six hundred dollars, they both had to work for at least five more years.

The third seamstress married an elderly man in poor health who died a couple of years after they were married. A Chinatown politician asked her to become his concubine. But she wanted to stay single and was enjoying only taking care of herself. She was attending an English language school at a local church and was promised a

*salesclerk job in a Chinatown tourist store when she com-
pleted school.*

*The fourth one, a widow of forty-five, had a man named
Wong Ging Wah living with her and her six children.
Wong Ging Wah was a penniless and shiftless Chinaman
who wished to be a man of leisure with plenty of time
to play big-shot and maneuver politics in the various
Chinatown associations; he needed someone like the
Widow Chong to support him.*

*Wong Ging Wah lived with Widow Chong and her six
children, all on welfare. The Widow Chong also worked
in the sewing factory and did not report her income. The
seven welfare checks and her income from sewing was a
good income for a Chinatown family and maintained
Wong Ging Wah's status in Chinatown's politics.*

*Widow Chong would only support and allow Wong Ging
Wah to live with her family, if he went to China to tell
his wife he was sending her back to her family. Therefore,
Widow Chong's status in Chinatown would not be that
of a concubine woman but of a wife, even though they
were not married by American wedlock standards. By the
other seamstresses, she was considered Wong Ging Wah's
mistress and not a wife, but they accepted her and her life
situation. If she married Wong Ging Wah, she would lose
her welfare checks and would have to support herself and
her children.*

*Lau Mae Shee, the sewing factory proprietress, was
American born in 1892. She learned to speak English at
a missionary school. An intelligent woman, she married
a schoolmate sweetheart and operated the sewing factory
as a subcontractor for a Mission District Jewish sewing
factory that contracted the work from downtown department stores.*

Her Brother Lau Yin's wife, Louie Wun Shee worked in the sewing factory, as a sort of limited partner. His family consisted of his tiny seventy-year-old mother … his wife, and seven children. They lived in two rooms at Sun Choy Lou, a tenement building. Lau Yin wished he was in better circumstances to make life more comfortable.

In her late thirties and after having seven children, Louie Wun Shee, his wife, … sewed with a three-month-old baby carried papoose-style on her back. There were three Lau children, six to ten years old … who came in after school for a snack before going to Chinese school. There were times, the ten-year-old … went to buy food for dinner, which was usually after Chinese school at 9:00 p.m. When there was extra work, sometimes dinner was eaten at the sewing factory.

Their fifteen-year-old China-born high school son shined shoes and delivered pre-dawn newspapers to help with the family income. The four-year-old daughter could usually be seen playing near the front door while waiting a few more months to be old enough to go to school. In those days, there were no day-care centers in Chinatown.

Because of the many sewing machines around at the rear corner of the sewing factory, Louie Wun Shee placed a playpen for safety measures for her two-year-old son, and a small crib next to it. Sometimes, Great-Grandmother Ning Shee brought Granduncle Herbert along and while she worked, she placed him in the crib. Other times, she took work home.

There was a two-burner hot plate in the back of the room for light cooking or heating up food the ladies brought for the day. The seamstresses also contributed to a pot to buy goodies like barbecued pork, steamed chicken, roast duck, and green vegetables cut into small pieces to be added to the large pot of slow-cooked joke, a rice gruel or congee. It was the usual luncheon for workers and children after school, because of limited cooking facilities. Sometimes, for a change, the seamstresses ate deem sum for lunch. Two large thermoses of hot water stood available to make ready tea. All the cooking facilities were placed on top of a 30" high four-door cabinet at the rear middle of the sewing factory. There was no refrigerator, and dishes were washed in the bathroom sink nearby.

The factory owner, Lau Mae Shee, had two sons. One was still in high school, and the twenty-year-old was working full time as a shipping clerk for a supply house. He still lived with the family and contributed to the pot to help his father go into the restaurant business someday. Ever since he immigrated to America as a child twenty-five years ago, the father had worked in Chinatown restaurants. For years, he had dreamed of being the boss of his own Chop Suey-American restaurant one day.

From 1926 to 1927, when we were still living at the Dupont Gai tenement, Great-grandmother Ning Shee worked at two Louie Jai Gai Chong, Laborers Sewing Factory, when Great-Grandfather Chow was out of town looking for work, and Great Great-granduncle Choie Tane was our baby-sitter.

One of the sewing factories was on Kearny Street next to the old Bella Union Theatre. Bella Union Theatre was known for its Can Can Girls during the wild and woolly Barbary Coast days when Robert Louis Stevenson hung around the hotels and bars in the neighborhood. As a small child, I used to quietly climb up to the mezzanine loft of the sewing factory and watch the Chan family eat their hearty meals below; I was envious of their wealth.

Another Louie Jai Gai Chong for which Great-Grandmother Ning worked was a basement sewing

165

factory between Jackson and Pacific in Stockton. The sewing factory was owned by a businessman who was reputed to have been involved with Chinatown's opium-smuggling-pool, which was facilitated through a Chinatown's diplomat woman who organized a sort of vigilante squad and co-operated with Police Sergeant Manion whose force got rid of drugs and the corruption of their living conditions.

It was common knowledge that opium was being brought in by affluent Chinese businessmen in cooperation with the British-controlled colonial Hong Kong and Shanghai underworld. They were the big wholesalers who dispensed to Chinatown's street dealers. Those dealers, just like today, were arrested while the drug lords made enormous profits.

A number of the Golden Triangle drug lords were reputed to be Chinese who fled out of China when the Country turned communist in 1949. Chinatown women were the ringleaders who supported Police Sergeant Manion because of the negative effect drugs had on their families and livelihoods.

As a child, I once picked up a can of opium at the Jong Hing Sewing Factory on Washington Street, across from Portsmouth Square; the Fung family's Buddhist Temple now occupies the site. One Chinese New Year, a female family acquaintance asked me to pick up a package from a seamstress at the sewing factory, and for ten cents, deliver it to another lady living in the apartment building next door.

The seamstress I picked up the package from was petite, young, pretty, and fair-skinned with soft, smooth hands and with a sing-song voice. I had a feeling that she did not work at the sewing factory because she did not look like any of the seamstresses hard at work in front of their sewing machines. On the way next door,

I got curious and opened the tobacco can. Inside, I found a tar-like substance.

Later, I described the substance to Great-Grandfather Chow. He told me it was opium I'd delivered; the Washington Street sewing factory was operated by Opium Czar Joe, who also operated a chain of dry goods stores in California.

I was warned that another kid had been picked up by the police for distributing opium in little packets folded into quarter-size cut playing cards, which he carried in his hip pockets to be delivered to buyers. Apparently, some fell out as he was taking out firecrackers to light up. Police officers saw the opium packets and took him to the police station. That was the first and last time I delivered opium.

In 1933, Great-Grandmother Ning Shee and I worked at another Louie Jai Gai Chong on Stockton Street near Jackson. The Hing Hing proprietor was an older, non-English-speaking single man who complained he was the sub-subcontractor to the sub-contractor to the White contractor for the department stores.

A dozen Chinese men were doing piece work sewing in this factory. Grandaunt Peggy Wing also worked with me as a child laborer. The jeans we worked on were quite coarse, heavier, and larger than the ones laborers wear nowadays. Grandaunt Peggy was eight, and I was ten years old. The boss sometimes assigned us to work that the adults did not like.

After the material came to the subcontractors, piecework was divided. The subcontractor attached stickers to each section of the jeans to be sewn together, saving the tags as a record of what the workers did. ....

Work was divided into the double-needle sewing parts, the inner seam and crotch, and the two side seams; I was a lock gwut finisher and a da moon pai, buttonholer. Lock gwut translated into lock the bone, which meant lock the seams. Lock Gwut referred to the doubled rows of sewing along the seams of the jeans. Da moon pai or "hit the door" openings, which, I presumed, referred to the six buttonholes of the flies and other parts of the jeans, such as the pockets. Making the single buttonhole for the waistband was the job workers tended to avoid.

Hing Hing Sewing Factory was open six days and closed on Sundays. On Saturday, ... in a designated corner of the store, a pile of pants tied into one dozen bundles were left. The flies for the jeans were cut in 2" x 9" and curved cut at the bottom. I could make the six buttonholes myself. I was paid one-and-one-half cents per dozen flies. The zipper wasn't used yet.

A single waistband buttonhole required both of us to work together.... We carried the dozen bundled men's jeans to the button-hole machine twenty feet away. To make the buttonhole on the exact spot on the narrow waist band, Grandaunt Peggy held onto the jeans so they wouldn't shift, when the knife came chopping down to cut the hole.

As a child, I wasn't scared of knives; I just wanted to earn money. As an adult, I've sometimes shuddered at the speed with which the one-inch knife came chopping down.

When done with our tasks, we re-tied the jeans in dozens and hauled them to the steam iron at the front of the store for the finishing work that required cutting out stray threads as well as ironing. For working Sunday, we earned a dollar and gave fifty cents to our mother.

During the Depression, movies ... cost five cents, and penny candies were still available. I wondered how we two little girls never made any mistakes in making the waistband buttonholes during the two years we worked at Hing Hing. What if we had cut the buttonhole at the wrong angle? What if we had lost a finger?

No damage to the hands was done. Ironically, the buttonhole machine was called the "Hand Hole" clothing machine. There is no record as to injuries incurred by children who were the primary operators of buttonholers.

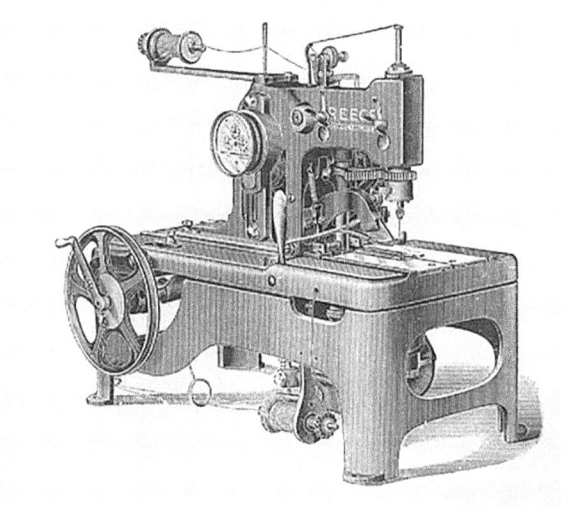

THE REECE BUTTON-HOLE MACHINE CO.

ILLUSTRATION OF REECE HAND HOLD CLOTHING MACHINE
Courtesy of Wikipedia Commons.

CHAPTER 24
Mol Ha Paw—Shrimp Shelling Women

Lennie found similarities with shrimping and sewing. Manual dexterity and working with the hands were but one of them.

The Pacific Heights matrons preferred unbroken pieces for their shrimp cocktails. Great-grandmother Ning and I were fired from Lincoln Shrimp Company on Commercial Street, when I was around eleven or twelve years of age for turning in underweight, shelled shrimps with too many broken pieces. We sat around each of the six tables in the factory. Each woman was given a weighted pan of tiny shrimps, three-quarters to an inch long, to shell. The empty shells were thrown into the middle of the table, and another pan was provided for the shrimp meat. Three-quarters of the original weight of the shrimp was required to be left after shelling. The See How Paw, Boss-woman, weighed the unshelled shrimps in an aluminum pan before handing it to us and weighed it after shelling. The See How Paw was furious and claimed she would lose business. She also insisted that I ate some of the shrimp, although I knew I did not.

I didn't want to eat the shrimp because I felt queasy in the very unsanitary conditions. I already had an upset stomach sitting next to a Mok Ha Paw, Shrimp Shelling Woman, who had several open sores on her hands, a runny nose which she wiped with the back of her sleeves, and dirty long fingernails with which to better shell shrimps. She kept picking up the shrimps I'd shelled to show me how poor a job I was doing. I could not grasp the shrimp-shelling technique, although the workers were trying to teach me. Another girl, a classmate my age at St. Mary's Chinese School, was very good at Mok Ha, shrimp shelling. To this day, shrimp cocktails I am still remind of the See How Paw and her Pacific Heights white matron-patrons.

During recess at St. Mary's Chinese School, I sometimes went along with the Mok Ha Nui, or Shrimp Shelling Girl, when she would lom fon, carry rice. She lom fon or picked-up left-over rice and other uneaten food from the Young China Newspaper company employees' dinner.

Young China was across the street from St. Mary's school on Clay Street. Before school, she had left a five-tier, 3" by 9" diameter aluminum container with a carrying handle at the newspaper company. I helped her empty all the uneaten food from the table. We carried the half-eaten food to her home and returned to school before the bell rang. The Mok Ha Nui family heated the left-over food after Chinese school and had it for dinner.

As part of their diet, some of the Mok Ha Paw also scrounge around Chinatown's produce market trash cans for discarded Bok Choy, a green leafy vegetable, to hang-dry out in their windows for soup. They also collected spoiled fruits and fermented them into wine, sometimes to be sold. They also acquired an innate fear of being harmed by the Bok Guai, White Devils; the fear of White Devils had forbidden them to venture outside the few blocks of core Chinatown. ....

Thinking back, I would be a good shrimp sheller. The thing I remember most vividly in comparing the shrimp shelling women to the seamstresses was that of being a good shrimp sheller. The thing I remember most vividly in comparing the shrimp shelling women to the seamstresses

171

SHRIMP BUYER AT HUNTER'S POINT C. 1930

Courtesy of www.foundsf.org.

*was that quite a number of the lady shrimpers still wore
the shiny black mar bo, hemp cloth, jackets with the frog
buttons up the front, pants, and clogs.*

*Seamstresses could also make their own inexpensive cloth-
ing and were comparatively better dressed and appeared
happier with their work. To the shrimp shelling women,
being able to sew was one step up in status as well as
earning power. Keeping their hands all day, year in and
year out, in wet shrimps caused painful rheumatism.*

*The black clothing of the Mok Ha Paw reminded me of
colonial British Hong Kong travel agency catalogs, com-
monly circulated with their pictorial advertisements of
Kowloon coolie farmers from a couple of decades ago to
attract White tourism.*

*When I first went to Hong Kong, in 1972, I took a tour
and was told that the Kowloon coolies charged ten dollars each person, Hong Kong money plus tips, to pose
with the tourists, as posing with tourists was strictly*

business. Today, hundreds of multi-story high rises and shopping centers occupy the land Kowloon coolie farmers once farmed. Farm-land-scarce Hong Kong has become dependent on the outside world for ... their food sources, including water from mainland China.

Lennie's cultural awareness was such that her journal included an insightful knowledge about Chinese foodstuff, along with memories and recollections about daily life. L K Lennie Lee also wrote about the cigar making business in her family and community.

CHAPTER 25
The Cigar Makers

OPTIMO FIVE CENT CIGARS

During World War II, when Grandfather Jing Loy Lee and I were young and on a tight budget, we sometimes took slow reminiscing strolls along Commercial Street, from Front to Sansome, once known as the Chinese Yin Hong, Cigar Manufacturing & Wholesale Center of San Francisco. The Chinese Yin Hong was replaced by one of four huge Embarcadero Complex Centers. Yin Hong was where Great-Great-Great-Grandfather Lee Bing You, and his Cuba, Havana Lee clan cousins' joint-ventured into the Lee cigar manufacturing businesses. San Francisco's 1876 Directory listed the Lee Clan's two wholesale and cigar manufacturing stores at 308 and 425 Commercial Street. The company's two cigar brand names were Ramirez and La Espanola.

CIGAR-MAKING OPERATION SAN FRANCISCO, C. 1869
Courtesy of Bancroft Library.

174

At the height of business around 1870-1880, as many as 8,000 Chinese cigar makers either worked at Yin Hong, were sub-contractors, or purchased tobacco leaves from Yin Hong to open their own cigar business with Spanish names. Among the Spanish names listed in the 1876 Directory were Arago, Aurora, Buena, Cerro Gordo, Decoto, Don Carlos, Isabella, La Espanola, and Ramirez.

Though most of the cigars made by the Lee manufacturers were sold to China, the use of Spanish names ... was for business reasons; Cuba, once a Spanish colony, was already known world-wide for the fine quality of its tobacco leaves and cigars and commanded a higher price.

The Hit Lo Houng, Iron Stove Canyon, and Lee Clan's cousins were already in the cigar manufacturing business and a branch of the Lee cigars, using Spanish names in Havana, Cuba, and San Francisco.

Great-Great-Great-Grandfather Lee Bing You and his Lee Clan cousin's company was the largest, with a total of 3,000 workers, including many families who made cigars at home. The workers were paid by piece work.

The Havana, Cuba, Lee clan ... partners supplied all the tobacco leaves to fulfill the Yin Hong manufacturers' needs. Some cigar businesses included several generations of family members working together with a storefront rather than under subcontractors. Parents, grandparents, and older children ... made cigars while the smaller children glued cigar bands and boxed the cigars. The best quality tobacco leaf buyers were laundrymen; the laundrymen spent their free time making fine Cuban cigars for goodwill to keep their laundries in business, most of which were located outside of the San Francisco Board of Supervisors proposed twelve-block Chinatown encampment.

During the height of the anti-coolie era, most Chinese laundries were located in the downtown-financial district, south of Market, and the Tenderloin districts, and many anti-Chinese laundrymen City ordinances were passed against the laundrymen to force them out of these three districts. These ... ordinances forbade Chinese cultural practices of carrying laundry in the street with bamboo poles, wearing their hair in queues, and living in large numbers in crowded quarters, even though their circumstances were because of lack of money and segregated housing.

Grandfather Jing Loy studied the old brick buildings, the remaining businesses, and people in the Commercial and Front area. The area had ... become a quiet, run-down old neighborhood with vacant lots and condemned buildings.

As we continued our walk a few blocks west and south into the busier financial-downtown district, Grandfather Jing Loy spoke about his youth. He talked about his experiences when he delivered custom-made cigars from nine to fifteen years of age to the nearby nightclubs, bars, and restaurants and how he made a number of lifelong White friends who gave him after-school jobs so that he could remain in America, when Great-Grandfather Lee decided to go back to China.

Mr. Bimbo, of the 365 Club on Market Street, gave Grandfather Jing Loy an after-school job as a kitchen helper and bar boy at his club; several of Mr. Bimbo's workers took him under their tutelage. A bartender taught him about Western drinks and the duties of a bar boy, and a chef taught him ... the art of fine cooking. When Great-grandfather Lee left for China in 1929, he allowed his son, Grandfather Jing Loy Lee, at age fifteen, to remain in the U.S. because he had a steady job and lived with several older Lee cousins.

As a delivery boy for Lee cigar manufacturing business, Grandfather Jing Loy was warned by his elders that the cheap Optimo Five Cents Cigar slogans was displayed at smoke shops. … It had the White unionists' victory slogans—an anti-coolieism slogan as a means of promoting White-made products.

Grandfather Jing Loy and I stopped when we saw an old "Optimo Five Cents Cigar" slogan in a small corner smoke shop. … It was semi-hidden behind several rows of horse-betting tickets, and it brought tears to Grandfather Jing Loy's eyes. The slogan reminded him of his permanent separation from the family. He last saw his mother, Great-Grandmother Wong Shee, his younger siblings, and … his father at fifteen when his father, Great-Grandfather Lee, retired back to China.

Though Great-Grandfather Lee was struggling in the cigar-making business to support his family, he was considered a rich man by pauperized Hoy Sun's district standards; children had been kidnapped for ten-dollar ransoms. Both of Grandfather Jing Loy's parents died during the 1937 Sino-Japan War, when Japanese soldiers invaded their village.

The San Francisco-Havana, Cuba Lee cousins' joint venture into the cigar manufacturing business, helped initiate several decades of anti-coolieism historical episodes. Local and national knowledge chronicled it as Yellow Peril politics or Yellow Journalism by the news media and special-interest politicians.

Soon racial-hate slogans such as All Chinese Must Go! or John Chinaman Must Go! became a national political issue. Chinese low piece-work wages, their willingness to work twelve to fourteen hours a day, and their increasing sales of Chinese American goods were said

to be the causes of White laborers' concerns and unem-
ployment. During the Wild West days, in many towns
with a Chinatown, such as Tombstone, Arizona, local
politicians made use of the anti-coolieism slogans to run
for political offices and won.

The influence of Yellow Journalism was so widespread
that even the Spanish names the Chinese cigar makers
used for their business and brand names became part of
the anti-Chinese issues in Cuba and Mexico; Ramirez
and La Espanola were also the business and brand names
of the Lee cousins in Cuba who supplied the tobacco leaves.

The Chinese cigar manufacturers' use of Spanish names
… caused difficulty in product name differentiation from
White-made products. Therefore, White unionists pasted
White labels across their cigar box lids. … It declared that
"the cigars herein contained are made by the hands of the
White Cigar Makers' Association of the Pacific Coast."

The Association held several trade assemblies and meet-
ings concerning Chinese using Spanish names for their
products. One day, during the 1880s, a number of the
White Cigar Association members, after being pro-
voked by anti-Chinese meeting rhetoric, invaded the
Commercial Street Yin Hong cigar business center and
stole and destroyed equipment and tobacco leaves. A sub-
stantial number of Chinese cigar makers fled out of fear
for their lives, and their business dropped.

Alexander Saxton (1971), a University of California,
Berkeley professor, researched and wrote about labor
and the anti-Chinese movement in California, "The
Indispensable Enemy," In the autobiography of Frank
Roney, an Irish rebel and California labor leader of
Denis Kearney's era, Sexton found time and energy to
record his experience as a member of the Workingmen's
Party in America.

We learned that Roney was locked in a bitter struggle with Denis Kearney to control the Workingmen's Party. He also focused upon the motto "John Chinaman Must Go! during the 1878 Trades and Labor Assembly" in Sacramento. The WASP, 1878, caricatured the Labor and Trade assembly as "The First Blow at the Chinese Question." Roney was involved with the debates and proceedings of the Constitutional Convention of the State of California, Sacramento, to add anti-Chinese clauses to the California Constitution of 1879, which included no right to vote or citizenship for Chinese Americans.

Great-Granduncle Lee, Grandfather Jing Loy's paternal uncle, said that Denis Kearney, a former convict from Ireland, was the most foul-mouthed and violent of those who led a number of the White Cigar-makers Association members to invade their businesses on Commercial and Front to demolish it, and beat up the workers—two Chinese men died.

Laws were passed that Chinese could not testify against Whites in court. During the height of the anti-coolie, anti-Chinese period, in the 1890s, Great-Great-Great-Grandfather Bing You's cigar business dropped substantially, from 3,000 workers to 500, when he decided to retire back to China during the 1890s. He turned over the management to Great-Great-Grandfather Lee—his son. The number of workers continued to drop to two hundred by the time Great-Grandfather Lee decided to close shop in 1929.

The unemployed Lee cigar workers migrated to wherever job and business opportunities they could find in the U.S. and Canada. Many moved to farming areas in the southern states, usually into the poorer migrant workers' neighborhoods. They built wooden kiosks along the farm roads and went into the grocery business, specializing *in the Mexican farm worker trade. They gave seasonal credits to the penniless Mexican migrant workers, which the Whites did not. They stocked food that Mexicans favored and learned to speak some tradesmen's language in Spanish. They collected the bills when the farming season was over, after the migrant workers got paid. They established an oral 'words of honor' trade with Mexican migrants since most immigrants could not write, read, or speak English. Some seasonal migrant workers became their steady customers and friends, coming back year-after-year, and they introduced other customers.*

In time, the former cigar makers were able to operate regular-size grocery stores, and in more recent years, their descendants operated chains, supermarkets, and other types of businesses.

Other unemployed cigar makers looked for work on the East Coast. In the beginning, they worked in hotel restaurant kitchens, laundries, farms, and whatever service jobs they could find. As years went by, many went into the restaurant, grocery, laundry, and export-import business.

When he was young, Grandfather Jing Loy identified a three-story red brick corner building on Commercial and Front as their last place of business. He assumed the larger original two buildings were destroyed during the 1906 earthquake. He rented the empty Commercial and Front lot or vacant land, from the White landlord, and rebuilt a three-story brick building on the same site.

It was a common practice for White owners with vacant lots to enter a build to suit agreement with the Chinese after the Great Earthquake and subsequent fire. Besides leasing the vacant lot, Chinese also paid to erect the building and lease it back from the property owner. Great-Great-Grandfather Lee made such an agreement;

he also provided cheap Chinese labor to help construct the Commercial and Front building.

At California and Front, Grandfather Jing Loy and I went in and spoke to an old-timer businessman he knew. In our walk, the man gave him the keys to his empty office building upstairs, and we explored. It was a five-story yellow-brick corner building with rickety, cage-like elevators; it was one of the many run-down old office buildings with vacancy problems since the 1929 Great Depression. The building was for sale, and the old man was willing to sell it to us with no money down, carrying back a large loan himself, but we wanted to buy a home we could move into.

Next, we walked toward the fishing piers and the Ferry Building. Several soldiers, on leave carrying duffel bags, asked directions to the Embarcadero Street YMCA, which was on the south side of Market Street. The sudden appearance of the soldiers reminded Grandfather Jing Loy of his brother, whom he last saw as an infant. His brother, a pilot for the Chinese Nationalist army, died when he was shot down in 1938 by Japanese soldiers.

To allow the slow-moving freight trains to pass, before crossing the railroad tracks, we stopped and waited prior to Embarcadero Street. Several of the cigar workers who also operated laundries at the Commercial and Embarcadero neighborhood still lived in the area; they and their cronies hung around the piers to fish during their days off.

Great-Grandfather Lee continued to lose money, though he worked long hours with few days off during the late 1920s, and, since he couldn't sell the business, he decided to salvage what he could from his savings and stocks and retire before going broke. He withdrew his savings of

$3,000 dollars in gold coins from a Montgomery Street bank. He raised another $1,500 by selling his storage of tobacco leaves, cigar-making molds, and various store furnishings to workers and to Grand cousin Lee Ngauk Loy, who wished to go into the Mai Hown Look Yee or Bribe the Blue Coat, police bribery cigar-making business.

During the early days of San Francisco Far Hown or Briberies were once an important mainstay for Chinatown folks to survive. They gave Far Hown to government officials and the police, as a means of survival. When Chinese Americans became more acceptable to work in the general society, this practice subsided.

Nonetheless, even during the 1940s, pay-off or bribery money wrapped around cigars was still common; gambling dens and lottery operators kept a payoff cigar box under their front counters. In the cigar box were cigars wrapped with twenty-dollar bills; when a policeman came around for the pay-off, those who bribed just handed a cigar.

Until Great-granduncle Lee retired in 1945 and decided to return to China, he operated a keno-like game called Gee Far in a Chinatown alley. With Gee Far, the players choose from a list of plants and animals instead of numbers as they do in Reno and Las Vegas. I watched the police walk in, and all Great-granduncle Lee said was "Have a cigar!" And the policeman responded. "Thank you," and was gone.

For a number of years, to compete with the machine-made Optimo Five Cents Cigars, Great-Grandfather Lee specialized in the more expensive handmade special-blend private brand Havana cigars, but he barely made a living. These handmade cigars required the finest and costliest tobacco leaves and highly specialized skills to create them.

Lee's Clan cousins ... had retired one-by-one, and gone was his steady source of prime quality, inexpensive tobacco leaves.

Grandfather Jing Loy, like other youths who spoke English, would rather go into other professions. He did not want to sweat over the cigar manufacturing business. Like most Chinatown businesses, such as sewing factories, Chinese cigar workers were still paid by piecework. Successful companies were largely dependent upon long hours put in by the owners.

Buyers of handmade special-blend Havana cigars became more and more demanding ... Some even came to the store to check the quality of tobacco leaves available and designated which cigar-makers were to make their cigars before ordering. Great-Grandfather Lee, who didn't smoke, was often appointed to make the cigars—cigar-making locked him into a life of drudgery. He actually detested the smell of cigars. But, to feed his family, Great-Grandfather Lee was forced into the business.

Of the 200 Lee cigar piecework workers left in 1929, only twenty or forty percent were skilled cigar makers whose craft could demand premium prices. Of those left, most were elderly and did not have many working years left. One hundred were unskilled cigar makers, and another sixty were semi-skilled, which totaled 160 trainees. Some of the trainees were middle-aged men and restless youths who couldn't find other work. Trainees rolled plenty of rejects, ... which added up to low counts of cigars completed; this affected their wages since they were paid by piece work. Rejected cigars also meant profit losses for the owners.

Grandfather Jing Loy often spoke about hilarious scenes that came about when Great-Grandfather Lee had limited cigar-makers to one only take-home cigar per day, because of stealing problems.

183

Grandfather Jing Loy recalled the dozens upon dozens of workers, each with a huge, unlighted, oversized brown cigar in his mouth, as he finished work for the day. Each worker showed the checker at the door his one only cigar as he left. Grandfather Jing Loy, whose genealogy name was Loy, and his cousins Ngauk Loy, Tim Loy, Gee Loy, and several other young Loy—stood outside the exit door.

They watched, laughed, and joked as each worker filed out the door after being checked for the one only cigar. A comical scene to watch the line upon line of small, slim-statured, brown-skinned, dark-clothed men in worn brown leather shoes pigeon toe single file out of the door with their heads raised high for balance. Their mouths were rounded and widely opened with enormous foot-long unlit stogies sticking out, firmly held up by both hands. The cigars appeared to be almost as large as their bodies. Some workers took one huge cigar home, unraveled it, and made it into a number of smaller cigars and sold them. Workers who didn't smoke usually sold their one only to stores in core Chinatown for reselling.

Grandfather Jing Loy did not want to go back to China with Great-Grandfather Lee because he still had nightmares about the series of bad experiences in hiding from kidnappers as a child. In fact, forty of Grandfather Jing Loy's Clan cousins rebelled against sailing to China, including a dozen still in their pre-teens. Some were recent immigrants who came as businessmen's sons, and the rest were native-born children.

The youth protested because severe crime and corruption problems still existed in many villages in Hoy Sun District. The place was still a poor district known for its kidnappers, pirates, poverty, illiterates, hooligans, clan clashes, slaves, castes, female infanticides, and longtime corrupt government problems.

184

Hoy Sun was well known as a bastion of anti-Ching rev-olutionists who defied and fought the Imperial Mandarin officials who viciously ruled under the old Ching Empire. The Imperial mandarins constantly raided the district and arbitrarily took locals to be beheaded. If not Imperial soldiers, it would be pirates who came in through Kwong Hoy Bay from the South China Seas. If they were not taken as slaves and concubines, whole villages and families, from grandparents to grandchildren, were anni-hilated. Many fled overseas, and some left for California during the coolie-traffic era.

Revolutionists disguised themselves and contracted as Coolies and Indentured Servants to escape to America. Chinese retirees who had returned were amongst an-ti-Ching revolutionists who fled to America disguised as coolies. They contracted themselves as Indentured Servants or Seven Years Slaves to the British colony White shippers of Hong Kong. Others were Shanghaied Chinese or re-leased prisoners shipped by White colonialists to build the railroad. However, most of the anti-Ching revolutionists disappeared into hiding.

Their comrades, once they landed on American soil, did not fulfill their Hong Kong Indentured Servant labor contracts. With the downfall of the Ching Dynasty in 1912 and the passage of time, the once-young revolution-ists, now retired elders, longed to return to Tong Saun or China to die. Others who had died in the United States returned to Tong Saun, their homeland, where their souls would forever rest in peace.

After much discussion, compromises were made between the adults and the teenage Lee youth who refused to go to China with them. Parents who wanted their pre-teen children with them, took them. Some parents insisted that their older children continue their education in China;

their conclusions based mainly on economic opportunities and racial problems in the U.S. They believed their children would get a more usable education, leading to better job opportunities in China. Western education was of no use for their children when there were no jobs available ... They did not want their children to become Joke Sings, or Bamboo Nodes, who were not Chinese or American culturally and were not accepted by Chinese or Western societies.

Some of the older children did not want to disobey their parents and left with them. Great-Grandfather Lee also exhumed Great-Great-Grandfather Lee's body in 1929 from the Hoy Sun Ning Yung Cemetery to be reburied in China. Great-Great-Grandfather died in 1927, and his body, still in the coffin, was taken to China and reburied in their Hit Lo Houng or Iron Stove Canyon, village family burial grounds. Great-Grandfather Lee asked his son, Grandfather Jing Loy, to withdraw his savings from a Montgomery Street bank and to carry the gold pieces to the ship in a leather satchel; gold was still thirty-five dollars an ounce, and the satchel was heavy as Grandfather Jing Loy recalled.

A recent stroll around the financial district, Embarcadero Center, and downtown smoke shops, showed that the Optimo Five Cents Cigar slogans were not on display anymore. Chain drug stores such as Merrill's were still selling Optimo cigars at an average price of three dollars for a five-pack; the cigars were much smaller than the ones I'd seen during the thirties. Front and Commercial Streets had become part of the Embarcadero Center complex of shopping malls, restaurants, offices, and hotels; a cigar store named Sherlock's Haven, at 1 Embarcadero Center, was established at the old-days Chinese Yin Hong or Cigar Manufacturing & Wholesale Center of San Francisco.

CHAPTER 26
Laundries

The end of the Gold Rush era, the completion of the Transcontinental Railroad, and continued emigration from China due to dire conditions, meant countless Chinese sojourners needed work. A return migration began when many came back to Chinatowns across the country and Canada. In the 1870s, the U.S. was in the throes of an economic depression, and unemployment was rampant.

Even if work was available, for instance, in restaurants, manufacturing, or construction, resentment toward Chinese workers often ended in violence. Another major problem was the impending passage of the 1882 Chinese Exclusion Act because it called for the deportation of all Chinese laborers, and exceptions to the Act were but a few—one was for merchants.

During that time, the enterprise that became prevalent was the Chinese hand laundry. The work was grueling, the hours long, and at best the pay marginal. Even though laundry work by men was not common in China, it presented an excellent opportunity for those in Gum San since White people were not deemed to do such work and yet wanted to wear laundered clothes for hygienic reasons. Another significant reason for entering the business was that not much capital was required. Equally significant was the fact that laundry owners were deemed merchants. This allowed them to bring wives and children to the country and thus laundries were a significant factor in Chinatown becoming a viable community.

Those who considered themselves of higher socioeconomic strata disdained the work, leaving it to those Lennie called illiterates. She didn't mean the term to be derogatory; she included herself in that category. It was rather an indication of how, in the Chinese community, there were those who considered themselves superior—a class above. Laundries gave the illiterates higher status.

AN EXAMPLE OF A CHINESE LAUNDRY FROM THE 1900S

Photo taken on location at Heritage Park in Calgary, Alberta, Canada, courtesy of Laura E Swan.

In recollection of these businesses and enterprises, Lennie wrote.

The Joun Sin Soun, Battling Scholars, or Fighting Hegemonies Tong war, as Chinatown folks named it, basically referred to two groups of people, the literate and the illiterates or lesser educated fighting over being better qualified to represent the Chinese community to White organizations.

These community conflicts were finally settled by arbitration among Chinatown folk. The two sides agreed that Chinatown's Soun Yee Gar, Businessmen status, should include men in the laundry business who tended to be illiterate or less educated and men in the importing and exporting business, who were generally better educated and wealthier.

Some of the Yow Chien Sar Chun, wealthy and haughty importers, were also known as key bribers and were in cahoots with corrupt politicians and city government agencies, which allowed them to openly advertise the sale of opium in the 1876 City Directory. Soun Ye Gar status allowed Chinese businessmen to bypass many of the Chinese exclusion laws ... such as bringing over their wives and children.

By 1876, as houseboys went into the laundry business on the side and also wanted a wife, Yee Sang Goon Mo, Laundrywoman, to help with the laundry and manage the job while he continued to work for White folks.

Chinese laundry workers were highly respected businessmen in the Chinese community. Many were considered ideal liaisons; they did the White folks' laundry, spoke some English, and lived in the Chinese community.

The many City ordinances passed by anti-Chinese agitators were political forces that Chinatown folks used to stabilize, organize, and build up their community's economy and further the education of their children. When City ordinances were passed against the laundrymen, they converted the ordinances to positive endeavors, to encourage all laundrymen to co-op, develop their own means to compete, and support themselves economically.

During the early days, Yee Shan Goon Hui a Laundrymen Associations was developed, when they pooled their meager funds together to purchase horse and carts to make deliveries. Many of their Clansmen laundrymen were employed as houseboys for affluent Whites, and they were able to cover a wider territory. In time, business increased and they purchased trucks. Eventually, as businessmen, they found ways to bring relatives and wives over to expand their businesses.

LAUNDRIES WERE A DANGEROUS BUSINESS

Besides occupational hazards, laundries brought other dangers. One of the primary reasons for the existence of Chinatowns was their safety in numbers, even though there was no guarantee of protection. A laundry business offered many opportunities for sojourners and Joke Sings alike, but huge risks existed. To be close to their clientele, the businesses were located outside Chinatown. This exposed them to nefarious characters found in the wild town of San Francisco.

July 23, 1877, a particularly gruesome event occurred. According to Wikipedia, the San Francisco Riot exploded.

> In the wake of the sandlot rally that continued over the next two nights. … but violence was snuffed through the combined efforts of the SFPD, the California State militia, and about 1,000 members of the civilian "Committee of Safety" group armed with hickory pickaxes[4]: 253 –254 np…

According to reports of the times, the riot claimed four lives and inflicted more than $100,000 worth of property damage on the city's Chinese immigrant population. …Twenty Chinese-owned laundries were destroyed …, the mob pelted Francisco's Chinese Methodist Mission with rocks, smashing its glass windows. The violence was taken to other places, and at 11:30 p.m., the mob arrived at a washhouse owned by Si Sow on Divisadero and Greenwich. He had recently purchased the business for $1,200—eight men were employed there. It was reported that several rioters entered the business, spraying the interior with bullets … and after ransacking the building, the mob set it afire. … Shot to death and left to burn, Wong Go's body was discovered inside.

That night, riots broke out again in San Francisco, with gangs gathering and being dispersed by the police, primarily south of Market. One group of approximately 1,000 men gathered in front of the San Francisco Mint and marched down Mission, threatening to burn the Mission Woolen Mills for employing Chinese labor, but it was well-guarded, and four laundries on Mission—between

Seventh and Twelfth—were sacked instead, as those businesses had been abandoned by their owners for the comparative safety of Chinatown.

It was reported that two laundries—one near Howard and Twelfth; the other at 1915 Hyde—were looted and set on fire. Police disrupted another group of looters at Bryant and Twelfth, who were about to set the laundry on fire. There were no reports of violence within Chinatown itself. (See Wikipedia Commons np.)

LAUNDRY WOMEN

Despite its dangers, Lennie recalled that there were many benefits in the laundry business for the community.

> *Not only was operating a laundry considered a respectable business in Chinatown but the Yee Sang Goon Mo, Laundry Man's Wife, was classified as See How Paw, Boss-woman. More ambitious laundrymen, Yee Sang Goon Bok, were known to select helpmates who could help them build their business and home-life, somewhat like the pioneer homestead farmers did.*

> *Both homestead farmers and laundrymen favored wives who could cook for farm hands or laundry workers as well as the family, bear many children, help with farm or laundry work, keep the books, and act frugal by canning excess food for the winter, or make use of unclaimed clothing left in the laundry, respect the husband as head of the household, as a strong-willed See How Paw woman.*

> *Just like the field hands of homestead farmers, Chinese laundry owners tended to hire men for labor-intensive work. Therefore, the Boss-Woman needed to be able to carry out instructions to workers when he was out making the rounds, to sell their produce or to collect and return laundry for the various laundry agencies.*

Many Chinese laundries hired a dozen or more workers because of the intensive labor involved. This was ... before large automatic laundry facilities were introduced.

During one hot summer day in the 1940s, I recall standing in front of a basement laundry with narrow stairways which led to Sacramento Street and watched with amazement how the Yee Sang Goo Bok, sweating with their shirts off, scurried all over the place to wash hotel sheets in hot, steamy chlorinated water which smelled from the street, all the while ironing the sheets on two eight feet long, three-foot diameter, revolving hot drums.

A few yards away, I saw several Yee Sang Goon Mo ... giving the finishing touch to the clean sheets; they used an eight by eighteen-inch white cardboard to fold and shape the sheets evenly by hand. The Yee Sang Goon Mo were all wearing open collar, flower patterned, cotton shirts with short sleeves. They also wore loose, three-quarter length dark pants and clogs without socks, displaying someone who could be a strong-willed See How Paw.

CHINESE FAMILY LAUNDRY, 1880
Courtesy of the artist, Mian Situ.

One wonders if women working in a laundry could be glamorous. Likely most were not but there were notable exceptions. For example, one of the most beautiful, glamorous women in history worked in a laundry. Iconic actress and film star Anna May Wong grew up in her father's Sam Kee Laundry in Los Angeles, where she folded and delivered finished laundry to customers.

However, she longed of escaping to become an actress. She eventually did but the Hollywood scene did not treat her well, and when she moved to Germany, Anna May Wong became an international star. During that era, Hollywood relied on White actors made up in yellow face to appear in Asian film roles.

ANNA MAY WONG & UNITED STATES QUARTER
Courtesy of the US Mint.

In 2022, Anna May Wong was honored by the US Mint placing her image on a quarter.

In that regard, Ventris Gibson, US Mint Director, wrote. "Our American Women Quarters Program honors Anna May Wong, a courageous advocate who championed increased representation and more multi-dimensional roles for Asian American actors" (National Parks Service, October 18, 2022).

Yet, despite being an international film star, Anna May Wong was required to carry identity papers to show on demand during the Chinese Asian Exclusion Laws.

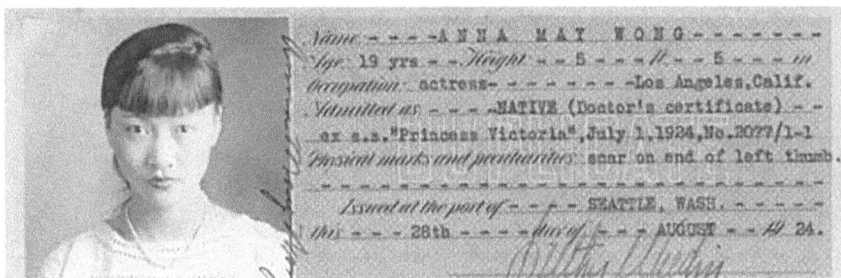

IDENTIFICATION PAPER

Courtesy of Department of Labor, National Archives, San Bruno.

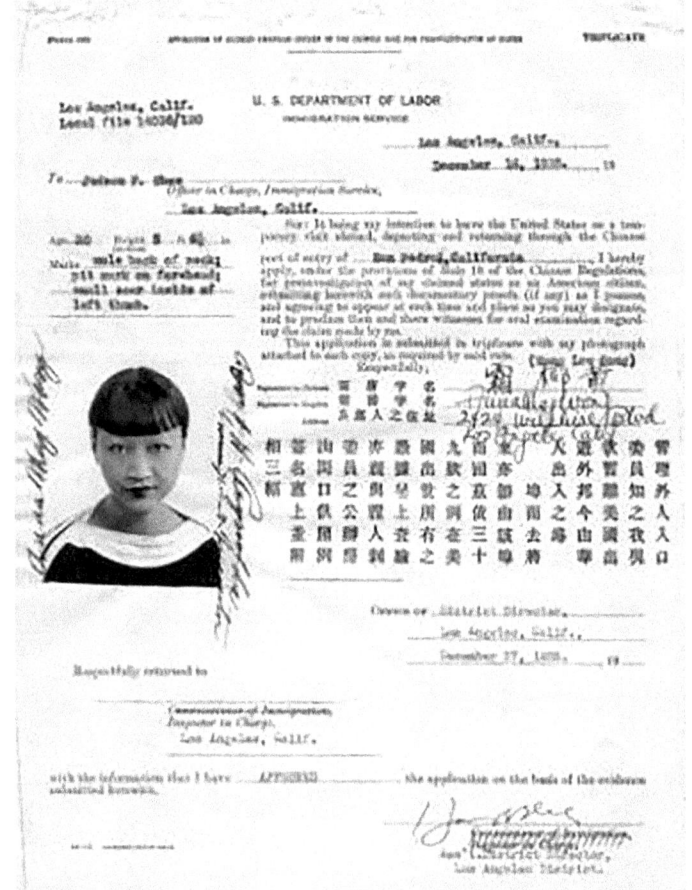

ANNA MAY WONG'S DEPARTMENT OF LABOR DOCUMENT

Courtesy of Department of Labor, National Archives, San Bruno.

Whenever she traveled overseas, Anna May Wong was required to make an application with the Department of Labor to get documentation to be assured of her return. The terms of the 1882 Chinese Exclusion Act and subsequent renewals called for the deportation of any Chinese person who was not a member of a merchant family. One exception was for natural-born citizens and Anna May Wong was a third generation American. Still, she had to exercise care.

She was perceived as a Barbie Doll, and because of all her achievements, the Clan bestowed its own accolade upon her: Anna May Wong was Badass. Along with others, one significant laundry person sought social change.

THANK A LAUNDRYMAN FOR YOUR CIVIL RIGHTS

Ask anyone, and they will likely assume a right to equal protection under the law; there are exceptions because as some politicians aim to dismantle the democratic system and substitute it with authoritarianism. However, if voters remain vigilant, the 14th Amendment of the Constitution gives everyone the right to be treated equally under the law. This provision was tested in 1886 by Lee Yick, a person who is most likely only familiar to those who know Asian American history. He operated a business called Yick Wo Laundry; a name familiar to every first-year law student.

In 1880, San Francisco passed an ordinance requiring that laundries operating out of wooden buildings must have a permit. On the face of it, it seemed reasonable, except that the overwhelming majority of those who operated in wooden structures were Chinese businesses. It was then that the City began to levy a $10 dollar fine for those who lacked necessary permits. Such a requirement was not imposed on laundries doing business out of brick buildings.

After Lee refused to obtain a permit, Sheriff John Hopkins arrested and jailed him. Lee Yick eventually paid the fine and was released, but the story did not end there. He filed a suit against Hopkins, asserting that the wooden building law was discriminatory. The case known as *Yick Wo v Hopkins* was litigated all the way to the Supreme Court, which issued a ruling that the law had been applied in a discriminatory manner. Most importantly, the court's wording in the amendment ruled that "persons" applied to everyone in the United States regardless of status.

In recognition for his efforts, Yick Wo has been acknowledged in public exhibits. For example, in a San Bruno display, an inscription about the case reads: "Supreme Court Evidence in the Case of Yick Wo ... filed with the Supreme Court of California on January 22, 1886." This view of Yick Wo Laundry at 349 Third Street—a site used to do laundry for twenty years—was presented as evidence of his violation of a San Francisco ordinance governing the construction of washhouses.

An appeal to the Supreme Court of the United States, found that,

> Though the law itself is fair on its face and impartial in appearance, it is applied and administered by public authorities with an evil eye and an unequal hand

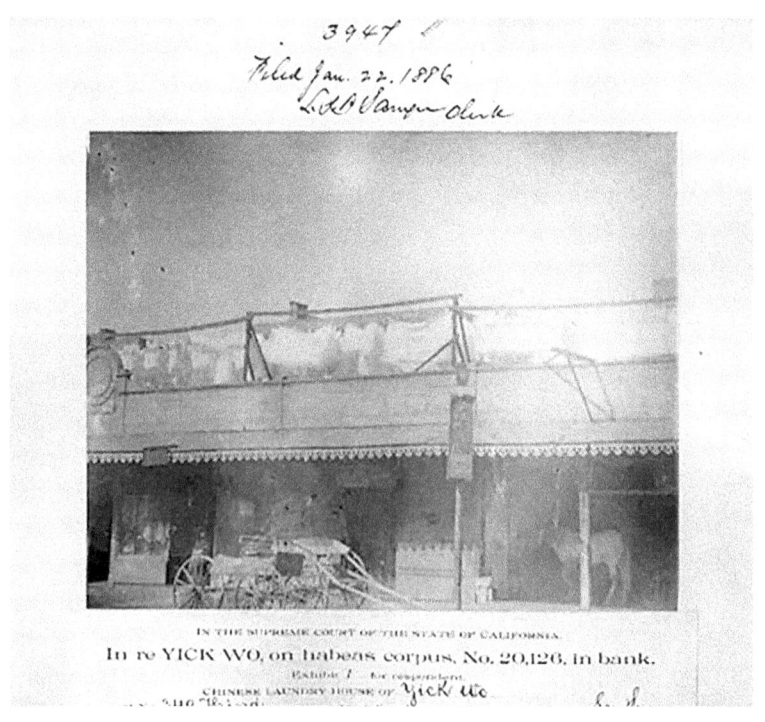

YICK WO LAUNDRY COURT EXHIBIT
Courtesy National Archives, San Bruno.

so as to practically make unjust and illegal discrim-
inations ... for persons in similar circumstances ...
denial of equal justice is still within the prohibition
of the Constitution (Thinking Nation, https://www.
thinkingnation.org, 2023/05).

Initially, the law did not have a widespread effect because the
White-dominated legislatures promoted discrimination. For instance, in 1896, the case of Plessy v Ferguson legalized segregation
under a concept called "separate but equal." Ever since, the Yick Wo
v Hopkins ruling has been cited in over 150 cases and has been a
landmark decision. Laundryman Lee Yick and his partner Wo Lee
were badass.

PART V

JOKE SING STORIES

THE CLAN WERE NOT THE ONLY ONES WHO
SAILED TO AMERICA IN SEARCH OF A BETTER
LIFE. THERE WERE OTHER INTREPID JOKE
SINGS WHO MADE THE JOURNEY. WHILE
DOING THE RESEARCH FOR THIS BOOK,
I CAME ACROSS STORIES WORTH TELLING.

CHAPTER 27
Pacific Grove & Mendocino

Pacific Grove is a beautiful, idyllic seaside town on the Monterey peninsula. I thought I knew the place well. Over several decades, my wife Lucretia and I vacationed there regularly. Besides excellent dining and beautiful scenery, I played the scenic golf course numerous times.

We enjoyed visiting the Monarch Butterfly Grove and Lucretia's aunt and uncle graves, who are buried at the local cemetery. I was aware there once existed a Chinese fishing village. However, until reading Lennie's journals, I did not know that the Clan routinely sailed from San Francisco to trade with the Chinese villagers.

The story of the Clan bringing Robert Louis Stevenson along for a visit in 1880 also sparked my interest in the town and those Chinese who lived and worked there beginning in the

COMMEMORATION OF CHINESE FISHING VILLAGE
AT POINT ALONES
Photo by Ron Lee.

mid-nineteenth century. During my research, I came across an article in the *Monterey County Weekly*, dated September 25, 2014, which celebrated the installation of a commemorative plaque telling an interesting story.

Part of the inscription immediately caught my eye:

> Because it housed single men and whole families with children, the village was unique among Chinese settlements of the time. Directly from southern China, pioneering women had sailed with men in seagoing junks (Commemoration Plaque, Monterey County Weekly, 2014).

Because of the presence of whole families, including children, the inscription was reminiscent of my ancestor's history. These were Joke Sings, not Sojourners. This was when I became aware that there were others with a similar history to my own.

A visit to the Pacific Grove Museum of Natural History was particularly informative. A display about Chinese inhabitants of Pacific Grove was on the main floor. The museum is a wonderful place to visit. While touring, I felt somewhat guilty about having passed it dozens of times over the decades without ever stopping.

PACIFIC GROVE MUSEUM OF NATURAL HISTORY
Family archives.

The space reminded me of the Palo Alto Junior Museum, which in the 1980s was slated for closure. Lucretia kept things going by gathering volunteers to design and build exhibits and organizing a variety of events. Thus, we are fond of museums.

During my research, the story of two incredible women came to light. Activist Gerry Low-Sabado (1949-2021) and her great grandmother, Quock Mui (1859-1936).

GERRY LOW-SABADO
Photo by Randy Sabado.

QUOCK MUI
Sabado family archives.

QUOCK MUI'S PICTURE OF WHALER'S CABIN
Sabado family archives.

While engaging this topic, I received an email from Gerry's husband, Randy Sabado. He spoke about the way Gerry became interested in family history. He said,

> To begin with, Gerry had limited knowledge about her ancestors and their contributions to the fishing industry in the Monterey peninsula. It was only by chance that she learned about the identity of a woman in a picture at the Whalers Cabin in Point Lobos. For most of her life, Gerry did not know about … their contributions to the fishing industry.
>
> After seeing her picture in the cabin, Gerry asked her mother about it because it was similar to her Grandmother's house on Wave Street. Only then did Gerry learn that the woman in the picture was her great-grandmother. This launched her quest to find out why no one in her family told her (personal communication with Randy Sabado February 6, 2024).

Why did her ancestors come to the Monterey area? How were they able to survive during the time of the Chinese Exclusion Act? The answers to these questions drove Gerry to tell this untold story to whomever listened. Thus, she became an advocate for remembering and recognizing the contributions of Chinese and other Asian Americans in the Monterey area.

Quock Mui turned out to be one of the most interesting women in Asian American Native Hawaiian/Pacific Islander (AANHPI) history, but her story had recently come to light. Quock Mui spoke five languages: Chinese, English, Spanish, Portuguese, and Indigenous Remsien. Her linguistic skills might have been instrumental in fostering understanding among diverse groups who lived in the area.

Quock Mui married Yow Hoy Jone and had six children. Mui passed away on September 27, 1936. Her story is the story of Monterey Chinese. Quock Mui, born in 1859, is likely one of the first females of Chinese descent born in California, and certainly amongst those in Monterey. How her parents first arrived is an interesting story.

CHINESE CURRENT EVENTS

The Clan were expert seafarers who crossed the Pacific Ocean multiple times, along with routine voyages between San Francisco and Pacific Grove over a period of decades. Their Junk featured three masts and a length of over 100 feet as shown below.

FACSIMILE OF FAMILY JUNK
Courtesy of Dreamstime.

In contrast, Quock Mui's parents were incredibly lucky to make their trip. Accounts vary, as to what exactly happened; however, sometime between 1851 and 1854, with the goal of reaching America from their Southeast China location, a group of seven intrepid fishing families set sail in their small vessels.

Noted historian Sandy Lydon (2025) expressed that their vessels were tiny, just thirty feet long, and way too small to attempt crossing the Pacific Ocean, a trip that would exceed 7,000 nautical miles. The other issue was navigation. Only two families made it, and one of them was Bo Quock and So May Loy—Quock Mui's parents—who shipwrecked off Point Lobos in Monterey. A local Indian tribe rescued them and treated them well.

A TYPICAL SMALL SAILING VESSEL
Courtesy of Scott Foresman Publications.

Although quite dangerous, it turned out that this wasn't an entirely impossible mission. There exists a current that circulates clockwise around the perimeter of the Pacific Ocean called the Kuroshio Current. In ancient times, it was known as the Black Tide, something to be avoided because getting caught in it meant no return. It turns out that vessels could catch the current and use it to sail all the way to America, and with expert navigation, one could make a return trip to China because the current ran clockwise and returned to Asia.

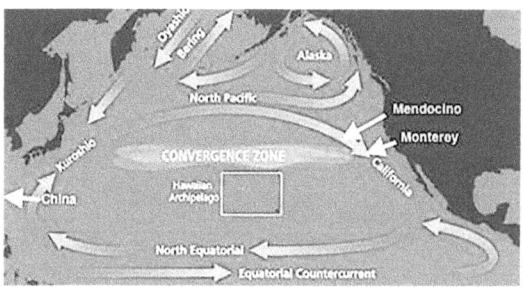

KUSHIRO CURRENT
Courtesy of Wikipedia Commons.

A vessel drifting on the current would naturally circulate from China to America in the North and back in the South. If they caught the current just right, the seven small vessels could reach Gum San. Unfortunately, their attempt had tragic consequences. Of the reported vessels that began the voyage, only two survived the journey. The other five families perished at sea.

Of the two that made it, one vessel landed at Caspar Beach in Mendocino. The other one, carrying the Quocks, shipwrecked at Point Lobos in the Monterey area. Members of the Remsien Ohlone tribe rescued them and got them established.

The lucky survivors brought expertise in fishing and a mutually beneficial relationship began. The Quocks built a cabin that still stands at Whaler's Cove. The family moved to Point Alones where multiple arrivals settled, with up to 500 residents, it eventually become one of the largest enclaves of Chinese outside San Francisco.

Primary fishery was squid, which was caught, dried on racks, then shipped as far away as China. Abalone was also harvested by Chinese fishermen, and later by Japanese American fishermen who were able to dive for the valuable shellfish. Squid fishing was done at night. This allowed Chinese fishermen not to get into conflict with Italian and Portuguese fishermen who were working in the same area.

The Museum of Natural History tells her family story and their arrival via the Kuroshio Current. Gerry's forebears were there from the beginning until the end. In 1940, her relatives formed Regal Fish Company which had a successful run until it was sold in 1973. The company was the exclusive supplier for the StarKist Tuna Company.

THE FISHING VILLAGE AT POINT ALONES

Courtesy of Pacific Grove Museum of Natural History (PGMNH) and Gerry Low Sabado.

GERRY LOW-SABADO IN FRONT OF A DISPLAY
AT THE PACIFIC GROVE MUSEUM

Sabado family archives.

We held a common understanding about our unique heritages and long-lost relatives until her mother told her the story. I learned about long lost relatives and their history from my mother. The difference is that revelations Gerry uncovered about Pacific Grove put her on a quest to right a wrong that would last the rest of her life. She also sparked a movement that continues. Her crusade was to point out and eventually change an unfortunate "celebration" known as the Feast of Lanterns that a Pacific Grove group promoted for 117 years.

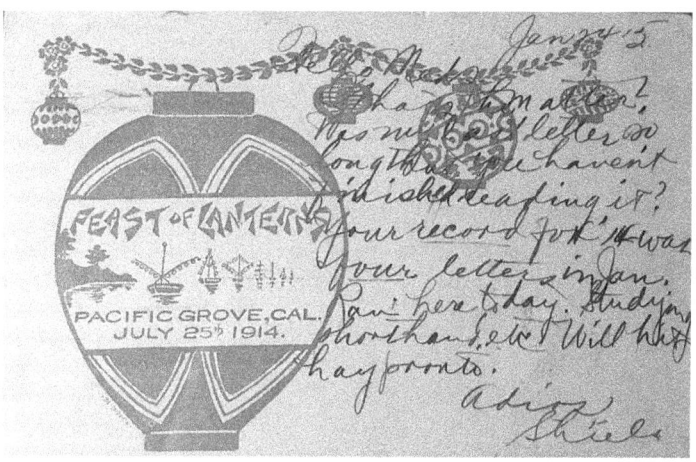

THE FEAST OF LANTERNS
Jane F., Yelp.com.

Pacific Grove began their Feast of Lanterns in 1905. The roots of the Asian themed program stemmed from the Chautauqua Institute of New York, an institution with methodist roots and no connections to Chinese history.

Tyrone Beason, Staff Writer at the *Los Angeles Times*, wrote in September 2022:

> Residents dressed up in Chinese-style robes of silk brocade and slanted their eyes with makeup and tape. Some even tinted their skin yellow. During a segment of the play that featured an arranged marriage, audience members would boo (Beason 2022, np).

This was a case of Cultural Appropriation or a euphemism for stereotyping. The use of an Asian theme actually was appropriated from the local community of Chinese fishermen who used a lantern technique to catch squid. At night, dozens of Sampans could be seen in the waters of Monterey bay with lanterns hanging from the prow or the stern, attracting squid to the surface where they were easily caught.

Unfortunately, when the event started, residents of Pacific Grove left out local Chinese. The village could have illustrated Monterey Bay history through with Pacific Grove presence and story. Sadly, a few weeks after the 1906 earthquake and fire in San Francisco, a puzzling blaze occurred at the Chinese fishing village completely destroying it. Thanks to Gerry and her allies' efforts, even when the Feast of Lanterns was set aside, an event called the Walk of Remembrance was organized to commemorate the presence of Chinese inhabitants.

REMEMBERING GERRY: A UNIQUE HONOR

The Monterey Bay Aquarium website describes Gerry Low-Sabado as one who created "Change with Kindness." In 2011, to commemorate Chinese heritage in Pacific Grove, in collaboration with other Gerry organized the "Walk of Remembrance," to peacefully replace a long-held, and unfortunate tradition that local town folks knew as the Feast of Lanterns. Her husband, Randy, said,

> Gerry struggled for over ten years advocating for changes and recognition of the Chinese Village ... She worked with organizers to create change with kindness but was mostly ignored. Gerry died in 2021.

GERRY'S NAMESAKE

In 2022, the Monterey Bay Aquarium named a chick after Gerry. The penguin now resides in an exhibit as an homage and reminder of Gerry. Sabado said that "penguins symbolize friendliness, community, and determination, three traits Gerry shares with penguins" (May 2022).

2023 WALK OF REMEMBRANCE
Family archives.

GERRY THE PENGUIN, MONTEREY BAY AQUARIUM
Photo by Randy Sabado.

IN REMEMBRANCE OF GERRY AND LENNIE

Gerry was 71 years of age and Lennie passed away at the age of 98 in 2021. Their respective stories described events that historians and academics rarely, if ever, document. Things would be different today, if intrepid souls such as Gerry and Lennie's ancestors had not settled in America and started their families. While Lennie and Gerry's personalities differed Gerry was kind, patient, and effective, while Lennie was direct, confrontational, and forward leaning. She was badass. In her own way, Gerry Low-Sabado also fit the criteria.

CHINESE IN MENDOCINO

Accounts vary as to how and when Chinese arrived in Mendocino. Stories range from crewmen who came ashore at Caspar Beach when a sailing vessel named the Frolic, shipwrecked in 1851. Some speculate that the arrival was a result of miners who went there to work in the lumber industry, after the Gold Rush.

An account by Lorraine Hee-Chorley, told another version, involving her great grandfather Chong Sung, also known as Joe Lee, which coincides with the story about Bo Quock and So May Loi arriving ashore at Point Lobos in the 1850s. Hee-Chorley recalled,

> My Great-Grandfather sailed from China on a sampan. As the story goes, there were a total of seven sampans that started out to come to California because of the California Gold Rush. We know him as Joe Lee, but in the historical records the spelling changed. He was a farmer from the northern part of Hong Kong. He and his brother started out in one of these sampans, and they sailed to Monterey, because of its Chinese fishing village.
>
> They got off course and landed up by Caspar Beach and discovered that there wasn't gold to pick up off the street. Chong Sung or Joe Lee, ended up at the Caspar Lumber Company. Then he came to Mendocino where he worked and with another

Chinese family and built the Temple of Kwan Tai, in 1854.

Constructed by Joe Lee the temple was held in the family but eventually was turned into a non-profit corporation. It is one of six original Chinese temples left. If it were not for Joe Lee and the Chinese labor force, the temple would not be where it is today. It was they who introduced the fishing industry to the town of Mendocino.

It was they who informed the community where the edible stuff was, introducing red abalone to main-stream society. They identified the abundance of fish that was out there, and the sea algae, creating a business. They dried the sea algae, ... the shrimp, ... and dried abalone; they saved the shells and shipped those back to China. It was a big industry.

CHONG SUNG (AKA JOE LEE) & DAUGHTER YIP LEE
Family archives.

Joe Lee and others settled in Mendocino and built the Kwan Tai Temple dedicated to the god of war. It exists today.

KWAN TAI TEMPLE
Courtesy of Lorraine Hee-Chorley.

MORE ON MENDOCINO COUNTY

In conversations with Hee-Chorley more history surfaced. She offered that at the height of the lumber industry, the town of Mendocino had between 500 and 700 Chinese residents. It featured a variety of herb shows, general stores, and restaurants catering to the Asian population.

Born in Mendocino, a noteworthy person was Look Tin Eli whose father operated a store in town. His brother was also a successful businessman. Look Tin was born, May 5, 1879, to father Luke Bing-Tai and Mother Su Wang who later had three additional children. At age nine, Look Tin was sent to China to receive an education. His return five years later was a portent of his significance to Chinese American history. Hee-Chorley said that his re-entry was denied because he lacked the necessary paperwork stipulated in the 1882 Chinese Exclusion Act.

In 1884, the family sued and prevailed when Justice Stephen Field ruled that persons born in the United States were citizens regardless of ancestry. This was a precursor to the landmark decision of the Supreme Court upholding the natural born citizenship clause of the 14th Amendment.

After founding the family store in Mendocino, Look Tin moved to San Francisco where he became involved in a variety of enterprises, from being general manager for a large Chinese emporium and bazaar, to banking, and the formation of the China Mail Steamship Company.

Look Tin's most noteworthy accomplishment was leading the redevelopment of Chinatown after the 1906 Earthquake and Fire. The decision to rebuild structures in an "Oriental" style dissuaded City fathers from relocating Chinatown out of its central location to the outskirts of the City; rebuilding was accomplished in two years.

BROTHERS LOOK TIN ELI & LOOK POUNG-SAN

Family archives.

A TRADE CARD FOR THE SING FAT COMPANY,
LOCATED IN SAN FRANCISCO, CALIFORNIA.

Postcard by Britton & Rey, Lithographer, S.F. Publishers of pictorial post cards.

PART VI

FAMILY TIES

ON MY WIFE LUCRETIA'S MATERNAL SIDE IS THE
LOUIE FAMILY, AND HER PATERNAL RELATIONS
ORIGINATE WITH THE CHANS. WHEN LENNIE
WROTE ABOUT OUR ANCESTORS, I BELIEVED IT
WAS FOR THE BENEFIT OF HER GRANDCHILDREN.
WHILE TRUE, IT SOON BECAME APPARENT THAT
THOSE TWO FAMILIES WERE SIGNIFICANT JOKE
SINGS. TO ELABORATE ON THEIR RELATIONSHIP
AS KIN AND PARTNERS, WHAT FOLLOWS ARE
STORIES ABOUT LUCRETIA'S KIN.

CHAPTER 28
The Merchant

The story of Louie Wee Lee—Lucretia's grandfather—is a classic example of merchant status importance. He was the founder of a store known as Shing Chong (pronounced "sing cherng").

JADE FON'S PAINTING OF SHING CHONG STORE
Courtesy of Pam Della, Executor of Fon State.

As has been established, during the Chinese Exclusion Era, every Chinese person was required to carry an official ID paper at all times. According to records, Louie Wee Lee came to America in 1900, as the son of a merchant for a store named Bow Kee in the Sacramento area. It's entirely possible he was a Paper Son.

After working at Bow Kee for some years, Louie Wee Lee returned to China, married, and had a son, Robert. October 1906, just after the earthquake and fire of April 18th, he came back alone. After the earthquake, the street was renamed Grant Avenue at the northeast corner of Grant and Clay Street, then it extends down the block to the southwest corner of Portsmouth Square. The building is at the heart of Chinatown, and the corner of Grant and Clay was destroyed.

LOUIE WEE LEE'S ID PAPER
Family archives.

The store site looked like this:

DESTROYED STORE SITE
Courtesy of OpenSFHistory.org.

After the structure was rebuilt, with the help of investors, Wee Lee founded the Shing Chong store in 1909. It became prominent in the most well-known corners of Chinatown.

Before the 1906 earthquake and fire, the main street in Chinatown was named Dupont. Old-timer Chinese still refer to the thoroughfare as Du Pon Guy—Guy means street in Chinese. With an interesting history, in the year 2,000, the *SF Weekly* named the corner the "Best Historical Street Corner in San Francisco," and wrote:

> Grant Avenue is not only the city's oldest street; its
> sand, mud, and asphalt have hosted a good chunk of

San Francisco's livelier moments, particularly on the block around Clay Street—half a block north from Clay, near 827 Grant, Captain William Richardson pitched a tent in June 1835 that he later replaced with the city's first wooden dwelling. Half a block northeast is the longtime city center Portsmouth Square. It was designed to face onto Yerba Buena Cove in 1839, by J. J. Vioget, city planner. Before becoming the Financial District, the site was filled in and clogged with clipper ships. When looking downhill one may visualize the vista's previous incarnation.

Cargo was unloaded half a block south (at Commercial) after it was hauled uphill from the sea wall at Montgomery Street. May of 1848, Mormon bon vivant Sam Brannan strode up and down Grant in all his finery, a vial of sparkling dust in hand, bellowing, "There's gold in the American River!"—letting the genie out of the bottle.

In 1851, the first St. Francis Hotel opened right on the corner. August of 1873, the first cable car chugged on its uphill struggle to Jones Street and immortality. That was the cable car that traveled up and down Clay from 1873 to 1942.

The trees in the following photograph are part of Portsmouth Square, and what would later become 800 Grant Avenue and the site of Shing Chong is in the center past the trees. The building had stores at street level. Later a hotel which became the namesake for the famous Saint Francis Hotel on Union Square, boasting it could provide clean sheets.

In 1983, the late Thomas W. Chinn, a noted historian and one of the founders of the Chinese Historical Society of America, wrote an article for the *Asian Week Newspaper* about Wee Lee and Shing Chong and Company. Some photos and an excerpt from the article follow.

FIRST CABLE CAR IN THE WORLD, 1873

Courtesy of San Francisco History Center/SF Public Library.

WEE LEE LOUIE (SECOND FROM RIGHT)

Family archives.

INSIDE OF THE SHING CHONG STORE
Family archives.

WEE LEE, IN FRONT OF STORE
Family archives.

The article summarized that those who knew him remembered Louie as proud of his store and often boasting that Shing Chong could provide all the necessities from birth to death, and everything in-between.

Some family members recall that, "During World War II, when the importation of foodstuffs from the Far East was impossible, Louie came up with substitutes such as Chinese brown sugar or wong tong (Chinn, 1983, np.)." His creativity was such that, "He turned his rooftop into a drying shed for such formerly imported items as dried duck or lop op, dehydrated cabbage or "chow got" and even salted fish or hom yee (Chinn, 1983, np)."

In this view of the Shing Chong Store, the person in front of the store carrying the tray on his head was a typical sight. He was delivering food to someone who had ordered from a restaurant.

Today, 800 Grant Avenue continues to be the central location of Chinatown. Even though Grant Avenue lost a bit of luster with the Pandemic, the location is now home to a $26.5 million project for

SHING CHONG STORE DURING WWII
Courtesy of the Neighborhood Project, OpenSFHistory.org.

TROLLEY IN CHINATOWN
Courtesy of the Neighborhood Project, OpenSFHistory.org.

TRAY MAN, EARLY VERSION OF DOORDASH
Courtesy of the Neighborhood Project, OpenSFHistory.org.

the Chinatown Media and Arts Collaborative (CMAC). Its mission is to provide programs that will revitalize Grant Avenue and Portsmouth Square.

GRANT AVENUE NEAR PORTSMOUTH SQUARE
Courtesy of Wikimedia Commons.

PARTNERSHIPS

At the National Archives, Meredith and Alison found a document that lists Louie Wee Lee's partners. It was odd to see many partners listed, as Wee Lee Louie owned the building. Still, during the Exclusion Era "partners" were protected from the 1882 Chinese Exclusion Act and not subject to deportation. They could freely travel to and from China and bring wives and family to America.

The family documents on the following page list immigration cases which referenced partnership in Shing Chong. Hundreds, perhaps thousands, owe their ability to be Joke Sings to that piece of paper.

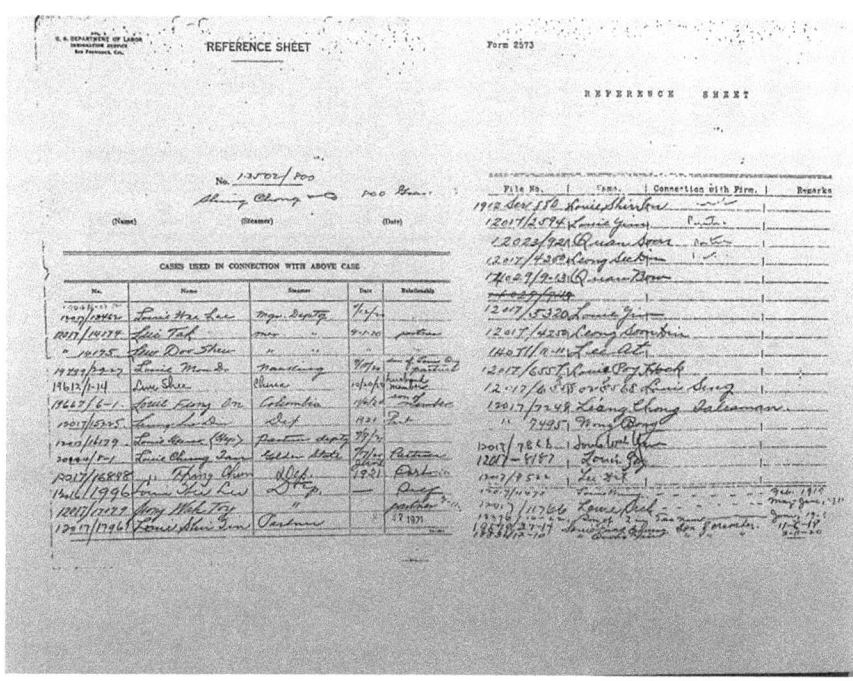

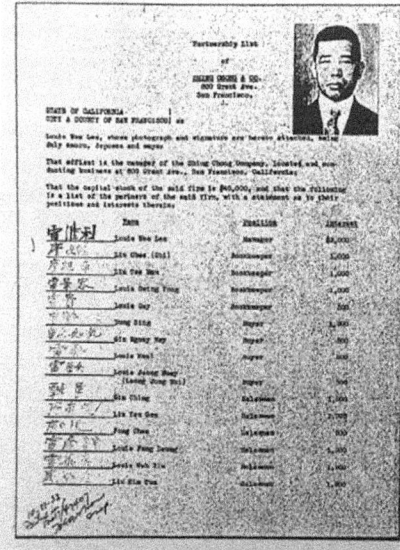

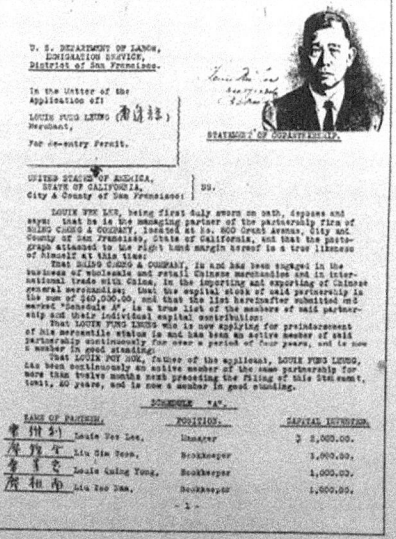

Whenever a member of the Partnership wanted to travel, a sworn document such as the ones above needed to be submitted.

FAMILY DOCUMENTS REFERENCING
PARTNERSHIP IN SHING CHONG

Family archives.

CHAPTER 29
High Tech Joke Sings

Innovations were brought or started by Chinese people. Before Silicon Valley, the earliest California high-tech enterprises started in San Francisco's Chinatown, when the Chinese Telephone Exchange began operations in 1887. It was formed through an agreement between Thomas Edison and Alexander Graham Bell, and named Oriental Telephone Company, because Edison envisioned international connections to Asia. Chinatown entrepreneurs formed their own company, the Chinese Exchange, which started in a small scale, with a lone switchboard operator, and a messenger who completed connections—it rapidly expanded.

CHINESE TELEPHONE COMPANY C. 1897
Photo by Charles Weidner, the George Grantham Bain Collection, Library of Congress.

In the photo on page 228, Bew Chan, John Chan's father, my wife Lucretia's grandfather, appears. The person in the background is Chan Yung Lai, John's grandfather and Lucretia's great grandfather. The operator is likely Yung Lai's son—he had twelve children, and Bew was one of the younger ones. In 1901, the exchange expanded to a three-story building at 743 Washington Street, but the building was destroyed in the 1906 earthquake. A new building was built at the same location with a new design that was very ornate.

VINTAGE POSTCARD, C. 1940
Courtesy of FoundSF.org.

After the earthquake, city officials sought to move Chinatown to a less desirable location. However, a number of intrepid individuals were able to keep the same location by changing the architecture to make Chinatown an exotic-looking location that would attract tourists. In spite of overt racism, Chinese people were an important part of the City's economy, particularly tourism, and Chinatown thrived.

CHINESE TELEPHONE EXCHANGE,
CHINATOWN, SAN FRANCISCO, USA
Courtesy of Chronicle/Alamy.

The new telephone building had an ornate interior and women operators dressed in exotic garb. Many of them were Chan's female relatives. As such, in addition to being an operating enterprise, the building became a major attraction.

In 1915, the Exchange participated in one of the major events in telephone history, the first transcontinental telephone call. John Watson called New York from San Francisco, and Alexander Graham Bell was on the other end. Also, Loo Kum Kee, founder and manager of the Chinese exchange, talked to a representative of the New York Chinese World. Later, Loo spoke to Wong Sue, a Chinese agent for the Southern Pacific Company in Boston. Operations continued into the 1940s. Several pay phones were maintained in the area, so there was wide access. The building later became a branch office of the Bank of Canton and remains a tourist attraction.

CHAPTER 30
The Chans

The young messenger, Bew Chan, in the telephone exchange picture on page 228, grew up to become a lifelong resident of Chinatown. Lucretia Chan's parents are John and Cecelia Chan. Grandfather Bew Chan and Grandmother Lau Shee had two sons and a daughter, with John being the oldest, then Haw and the youngest being George. Born in 1915, John who was Lucretia's father, appears in the photograph below with his parents.

Bew was a professional musician who played Chinese instruments. He frequently was away playing Chinese operas at different venues in California. Unfortunately, Lau Shee died early. The three children were tantamount to being orphans. When Bew was away,

BEW CHAN, LAU SHEE & BABY JOHN CHAN, C. 1916
Family archives.

his sisters often cared for the children from the family home on Jackson Street. However, the "aunties" were all busy because they were operators at the Chinese Telephone exchange, which was a twenty-four-hour operation. The decision was to send the two younger children to live in orphanages. George was sent to live at Chung Mei Orphanage across the Bay in Berkeley. Haw lived in a female-only residence called Gum Moon Home on Washington Street. John, the oldest at eight, stayed with relatives, but he looked out for the welfare of his brother and sister.

As a boy, John crossed the bay to Berkeley every Sunday to pick up George and bring him over for a family dinner, then escort him back to the orphanage. Despite such humble and modest beginnings, the siblings all grew up to be just fine. An industrious and artistic person showed constant interested in new things, and he was a civil engineer for CalTrans, the state transportation agency. He did the layout design for many of the highway interchanges in Santa Clara County.

The manager of Gum Moon Residence was Lucretia Kirk who subsequently adopted Haw Chan. Haw graduated from UC Berkeley and then attended the University of California School of Medicine in San Francisco. There, she met Edmund Jung, whom she would marry. Haw had a long career as a pathologist. Edmund was an internist for the VA Hospitals.

However, the Chans would become examples of how even exemplary citizens had to fight discrimination. Haw's husband, Dr. Edmund Jung, is such an example. Late in his career at the VA Hospital in Martinez, a new administrator by the name of Michael Geokas arrived. He was an outright racist who tormented Jung with inappropriate slurs and impediments to his work. Matters were complicated at the Veteran's Administration with the tepid response given to complaints about the issue. Rather than take things quietly, Dr. Jung filed a suit against Geokus for racial discrimination and against the Veterans Administration for lack of response.

After a long, protracted legal battle and with the help of protests by a group called Chinese for Affirmative Action, he prevailed. Jung also advocated for other minority physicians and is well remembered for his nearly six-years of battle with the biased administrator.

George had a long career at the State of California Agriculture Department. As a pastime, he was a lighting and sound engineer for Sacramento's Civic Light opera Company.

HOME AT LAST

John and Cecelia Chan were featured in a May 2018, PBS documentary entitled *The Chinese Exclusion Act*, showing how the Chinese overcame the trials and tribulations of the discriminatory Chinese Exclusion Act of 1882. The program asserted that after the war, and by the '60s and '70s, Chinese Americans had become valued members of American society.

The picture below is cropped from the end of the film, most likely taken by Dr. Edmund Jung, John's brother-in-law and an amateur cinematographer. It shows the Chan family strolling past their architect-designed San Mateo home and purported to illustrate how Chinese families became part of the American dream. The scene was shot in 1956—he was successfully middle class and had achieved much, but there is a backstory.

JOHN CHAN AND FAMILY AT THEIR SAN MATEO HOME
Family archives.

John was a young man ahead of his time. In 1950, he decided to move his family out of Chinatown because Lucretia was constantly getting sick, and the idea was to relocate in the more moderate Mediterranean-like climate of the less crowded San Mateo.

When he went to look for housing, John was initially disappointed. Realtors in the area indicated to him that there was a restriction barring Chinese from acquiring a home west of El Camino Real. Undeterred, John started driving around the west side. Going up a hill to an area known as Hillsdale, he came upon a Chinese gentleman who was gardening in front of his house. John inquired how he could have a home in the area. The gentleman, Donald Wong, said he was part of a family flower-growing operation but that they had become wholesale distributors and no longer needed their fields. Instead, they built homes and told John that his brother-in-law had just finished a house for sale. John took a look and liked the home immediately, so he bought it. A bank loan was unlikely. He sold his interest in the Jackson Street flat he shared with his extended family, borrowed money from others, and then, in addition to working as an Engineer at Caltrans, for more than a decade, he spent evenings as a waiter at Trader Vic's restaurant to liquidate his mortgage. He provided a very comfortable living for his family.

Lucretia recalls the area was so new that past their house was nothing but a cow pasture. John Chan deserves recognition. In a xenophobic era that promoted open housing discrimination and de facto segregation, he bought a brand new, beautiful, architecturally designed home that was located the furthermost west of El Camino Real that one could live in San Mateo—well done, young man!

Today, sixth and seventh-generation descendants continue to live in the City. The Joke Sing tradition continues. It is likely that any immigrant, no matter their country of origin, whose family has been in the United States for more than a generation, had a Joke Sing somewhere along the line. Here's to them all.

IN THE END

One could get the impression that the Clan and other relatives routinely skirted the law. However, their actions were more than simply a criminal enterprise. The Chinese were harshly treated and also exploited. In addition to xenophobia, there was financial exploitation. An example may be found in https://www.pbs.org/wgbh/americanexperience/features/goldrush-chinese-immigrants/:

> By 1870 there were 63,000 Chinese in the U.S., 77% of whom were in California. That year, Chinese miners contributed more than $5 million to the state's coffers through the Foreign Miners Tax, almost one quarter of state's revenue.

It didn't end with the government. The Huigans provided lots of services but also profited mightily.

I have concluded that my ancestors may have been law violators. However, they were following a tradition that dates to the beginning of the country. The founding fathers were also scofflaws to British rule as evidenced in their motto of "No taxation, without representation."

The Clan no doubt felt the same way. They were part of an economic engine for the country without citizenship rights. Kudos to them and others who survived, then thrived regardless. Their stories allow me to conclude that there were Badass Chinese people who had the ability to deal with difficult situations, overcome them, and survive.

EPILOGUE
A Woman of Courage & Determination

L K LENNIE LEE
Family archives.

In January 2021, after a Covid Pandemic quarantine period, I moved Lennie from an assisted living facility she had occupied for a couple of years and took her home to the Richmond District of San Francisco. As one could well imagine, Lennie was very happy to make the move. The facility she was in did a nice job of care and social activities, but there is no place like home. We, Alison and Meredith, my daughters, and I were lucky that a longtime caregiver we knew, Mougna (pronounced Mona), was available for Lennie.

There wasn't as much to do, living at home, but she basically didn't mind. L K Lennie Lee's flat overlooked a Safeway parking lot, and for hours she would sit by the window watching all that went on. Also, to follow current events, she watched television, especially the news. Meredith and Alison, who live in the City, carried out necessary errands.

Except for health professionals, because we wanted to be cautious about exposure to Covid-19, we didn't encourage visitors. Every week for ten days or so, I would come over and take Lennie out for a drive. Mougna came along and helped.

Unless she had a medical appointment, which was not often, Lennie enjoyed driving around the City and taking in the sights. We'd have lunch, drive some more, then return home. Getting her back was not an easy task. She lived on the top floor of a typical San Francisco flat. There were twenty-seven steps from the street to her floor. Having lived there for sixty years, where she had gone up and down daily, she insisted on climbing the stairs. Still, we instructed Lennie sit in a wheelchair and get carried up and down.

During our drives, Lennie was unusually quiet and contemplative. I could tell, though, that she was interested in the sights. Deciding where to go was a matter of thinking about the places she would like to see. In my view, any place with the name "China" in it was a candidate. Thus, Chinatown, China Beach, and China Basin became our destinations.

I tried to pick scenic routes in between. She particularly enjoyed riding through Lincoln Park Golf Course, which was on the northwest tip of the San Francisco Peninsula, then down along El Camino Del Mar, where we would pass China Beach. Views of the Golden Gate were spectacular. Ironically, we never drove to the Beach itself, because I did not know the significance of the location for her. We also drove through the Presidio, along Marina Boulevard past Crissy Field and the Marina Greens, and on to Chinatown. Then we went to the Embarcadero on the city's east side, past the Ferry Building, and down Third Street to China Basin. After that, we returned home via Clement Street, now the "new" Chinatown.

As we passed each of the China locations, Lennie leaned forward just a bit, turned her head to follow the sights, and then leaned back. I'd ask if she wanted to stop, but she didn't. Our only stops were for lunch. Sometimes, I'd parked and get takeout lunch to bring to the car. Getting out to go to a restaurant was difficult and tiring.

November 2021, I got a portentous telephone call from Mougna. She let me know that Lennie was listless and unable to talk. I told her to call 911. An ambulance came and took Lennie to the Emergency Room where I was later informed, she had suffered a sudden stroke.

Always the planner, "Grandma" had left instructions that she did not want any "heroic" measures. We set up Hospice Care and brought her home. A few days later, L K Lennie Lee passed away quietly. For me, our driving around took on a poignant meaning, not aware if my mom knew her time was short.

Later, after reading the working manuscript, I came to the realization that the places we visited had significant connection and meaning to the story of our Clan and its connection to others. It was very nice, though a bit sad, to know I was able to take her to those nostalgic spots. Kudos to L K Lennie Lee. She truly was an outstanding Joke Sing.

Inspired by my mother's anthropological imagination, and wishing to share the oral histories she collected, I unraveled the ancestral odyssey of becoming American. Through Lennie's writings about our ancestors and those kin who were part of the Clan to which I am extremely proud to belong, it is my hope to have inspired readers to search for their ancestors, community connections, and personal roots. Also, remember that at times, it will be necessary to be "badass."

SOURCES AND REFERENCES

Armentrout-Ma, L. E. 1972. "Chinese and GGNRA, 1849-1949: Guests of Choice, Guests of Necessity,

Cannery Row Historic Newspaper, Winter/Spring 1995-1996 (copyright 1995 by the Cannery Row Marketing Council; used with permission).

Kemp, et al., "Chinese Start Monterey Fishing Industry, 1995-2005)," Chinese Start Monterey Fishing Industry, Monterey County Historical Society, Inc.

Literature.com, STANDS4 LLC, 2025. *"Across the Plains, with Other Memories and Essays Books."* Accessed February 16, 2025. https://www.literature.com/ebook/across_the_plains,_with_other_memories_and_essays_614.

Lee, Lennie L. K. Memoires and journal notations document the lived experience of Chinese ethnics in various Chinatowns, providing a perspective of San Francisco's Chinatown as an insightful and committed citizen who had and maintained invested relationships with her community. Her words are italicized to identify her voice as she narrates her and her community experiences growing up and coming into adulthood in San Francisco's Chinatown.

Lydon, Sandy, 1985. *Chinese Gold: The Chinese in the Monterey Bay Region* (Capitola Book Co., Capitola, CA).

--------- 2005. "The Chinese Fishermen in the Monterey Bay Region," Sandy Lyndon's *Central Coast Secrets* np. www.sandylyndon.com.

Stevenson, R. L. 2011. *Robert Louis Stevenson. Leather-Bound Classics.* San Diego, CA: Advantage Publishers Group.

Swope, K. M. (2014). *The Military Collapse of China's Ming Dynasty, 1618-44*: London, Routledge.

Shaping San Francisco, 25 Years. White-buyers-at-HP-shrimp-dock2837.jpg. July 2411.(Retrieved February 19, 2025. https://www.foundsf.org/index.php?title=File:White-buyers-at-HP-shrimp-dock_2837.jpg.

Takaki, R. (1994). *From Different Shores: Perspectives of Race and Ethnicity in America,* 2nd Edition, Oxford University.

_____ (1993). *A Different Mirror: A History of Multiculturalism in America.* Little Brown & Co; (June 1, 1993).

Wikipedia The Free Encyclopedia, History of China; *China Knowledge, a comprehensive online encyclopedia of Chicana,* from Ulrich Theobald, and *The Berkshire Encyclopedia of China on Oxford Reference,* and *China Rediscovers its Own history,* a lecture by Yu Ying-Shih.

L K LENNIE LEE and RON LEE were born and raised in Chinatown, San Francisco, California. They both held careers as public-school teachers and later become real estate investors. They were leader and activists in their communities and fought for educational and civil rights. An avid reader, and an organic intellectual and self-taught researcher, L K Lennie Lee amassed an extensive oral history, as well as compiled narratives from young and old, to make observations of life in San Francisco's and other Chinatowns, taking the narrative beyond the facade of tourism. L K Lennie Lee collections of oral histories and transcribed conversations, document and bring to life the histories of her times, resulting in the production of *SOJOURNERS to JOKE SINGS TALES OF CHINATOWN & BEYOND*.

Ron Lee, inspired by his mother's career, was also a life-long educator. Like Lennie Lee, Ron Lee was an activist leader who continues to be involved in a variety of issues concerning Asian American Native Hawaiian and Pacific Islanders' rights. While he never imagined writing a book about the legacy of his ancestors, inheriting a treasure trove left by his mother, who directed him to write a book along with his two daughters and nephews, it took three years to produce. This collaborative endeavor documents the legacies of their ancestors. In that process, L K Lennie Lee also recorded her own lived experiences, yielded a living history, that unearthed the legacies of a Chinese diaspora that spreads from San Francisco to Pacific Grove, Mendocino, Stockton, Sacramento, and Tombstone, Arizona, along with other places where Chinatowns were established.